A

Beth Stephenson's

Americana

Beth M Stephenson

With Gratitude

To patriots who have sacrificed for their love of this great nation: both those who are known and those who are not.

Only In America, God bless it!

Thanks to my sweetheart Jeff for assembling and editing and taking some of the photographs in this second-year volume of Americana. May God bless him!

Beth M Stephenson

Table of Contents

Beth M Stephenson

Forward

Dear Americana Readers,

In a recent election year, I listened to all the hate and smear and ugliness as people each claimed that they knew better than anyone how to fix America.

I have travelled all over America and its territories and know that though we haven't yet solved all of America's problems, this is truly a blessed land, a land of promise and opportunity.

I know there are haters and screamers but there are kind, generous, courageous Americans all over this land.

I know that there is injustice and darkness in our history, but there is much that is noble, heroic and even divine.

That's Americana! Everything and anything that is good in America.

In this second volume from the columns published in The (Oklahoma City) Oklahoman and the Provo Daily Herald we revel in the goodness of this blessed land.

Only in America, God bless it.

Beth M Stephenson

Chapter 1   She Didn't Do It for the Money

There's something special about the Cast Iron Grill in Lubbock, TX. It's not just the luscious pies on display near the door. Nor is it the Christian/Americana décor. It's not even the friendly service or the tasty food. There's a spirit about the place that was hard for me to define until I heard the owner's story.

Theresa Stephens was a stay-at-home mom. Her husband, Shelby provided well for her and their two sons. But the boys were teenagers and she wanted to do something more. She set a goal to make a positive difference in somebody's life every day. She prayed and thought and waited for an idea that would provide a way for her to keep her goal.

When she heard that a little restaurant in downtown Lubbock was for sale, she went to look at it. She'd never thought of opening a restaurant, but the place felt right. It seemed like at last she had an answer to her prayer. She had no idea how a diner would translate into that, but she moved forward. "I just trusted my Heavenly Father to lead me," she remembers.

They bought the grill and spent the next few months experimenting with recipes. She'd never baked a pie until she decided to sell them. She admits she made dozens, maybe even a hundred flops until she was confident her recipes were so special that customers would want to buy them. For someone who had never made a pie, Theresa was a fast and fabulous learner.

 Though the city of Lubbock had addressed some elements of revitalization ten years earlier, they had concentrated on the area around Texas Tech University. That part of town had been transformed into an inviting artsy area, sure to be attractive to visitors. But the downtown where Theresa's new venture was located, was still a bit rundown. The Cast Iron

Grill paid its own way from the beginning. The cherry on top was that she never had to borrow money to make it work.

"When we started in 2007, I never dreamed we'd be where we are today. My favorite compliment is when people say they come here not just for great food and service, but because they are treated like family," she explained. The Grill has plenty of regulars that come to relax and chat. Some come as often as several times a week.

After Theresa had been in business for 2 ½ years, she started taking a small salary. Business grew steadily and Lubbock officials noticed that a business in the older part of town was not only thriving but growing. The city moved forward with downtown redevelopment projects. The decades-old Cactus Theater was sold and the new owners immediately upped the ante with an excellent house band and landing high profile performers.

Other upscale and midscale restaurants began appearing in the neighborhood attracting new customers into the district and further polishing the feel of Lubbock.

After doing business for about 5 years, Theresa moved The Cast Iron Grill to a bigger home, still in downtown Lubbock. She started thinking and praying about what to do next to increase the lives she touched. About that time, she heard about St. Benedicts chapel, a non-denominational group that cares for the homeless. She looked into it and knew it was right for her business. "Feeding the hungry is what we're all about."

The Cast Iron Grill is the only business that participates in the St. Benedict Chapel ministry. Each Monday, she and her family and employees cook the meal and then carry it over to be served. At first, some friends helped the Stephens' serve the meals too, but lately a group of volunteers receive the food and serve it for them. "We've been so blessed to be part of filling that need. I love that we can give back to our wonderful community."

"Everything that has happened is just a miracle," Theresa says. "The Cast Iron Grill has grown and my husband, (Shelby) and two sons (Taylor and Branum) work with me, so it has become a family business. People tell me that they feel the love and joy of this place. That's what I love most of all: when people have an emotional response to it.

Yes, it's hard to explain how the spirit of a restaurant made it special. The fact that she started The Cast Iron Grill so she could make the world a better place is the sweetest part of all.

Only in America, God bless it.

Beth M Stephenson

Chapter 2   Kindness Stops the Stone Throwing

Vicki Shell loves to rock hound. On a recent visit to Washington State, she and her brother, Mike Plumb, spent an entire day mining a creek bed for special stones. Among the crystals and hag stones, they had found some first rate carnelian agates.

By the end of the day, their clothes were soaked and muddy and their boots were full of water. Bits of blackberry brambles tangled Vicki's hair. Their muscles were already sore from bending, lifting and digging the semi-precious stones. Mike decided to stop at the store on the way home and buy a bucket of chicken for the family.

Vicki declared herself too unsightly to go into the store with him, so she waited in the car.

Before long, she noticed a young boy, seven or eight years old, running out of the store into the parking lot. He ran up and down the cement divider. At first, Vicki thought he was just playing, burning off some extra energy.

But after a moment, his mother rushed into the parking lot, calling him. She soon spotted him, darting between parked cars, running away from her.

Vicki's first thought was, "That little brat! That mom needs some help! I'm a fast runner, and I can catch him for her." But then she thought of her appearance. Looking like the Bride of Sasquatch, she didn't want to scare the mother or the child.

The little boy started picking up rocks from the median and throwing them at his mother. He had a deadly aim, hitting her almost every time. Vicki heard the rocks pinging off of the surrounding cars.

The mother retreated, watching the boy. She pulled out her cell phone and called someone for help. The boy advanced, pelting her and the nearby cars.

Inspiration struck Vicki. This was not just a naughty kid. There was a reason for his serious distress. Vicki thought of the bucketful of treasure in her backseat and got out of the car. Her thoughts raced. Would the mother tell her to mind her own business? Would the boy turn on her? Would he grab her rocks and use them as fresh ammunition?

Vicki explains that she has always been tenderhearted. "I've always tried to help someone in distress, look out for the underdog or befriend someone who is lonely."

"Hey, I want to show you something," she called to the boy. She mustered her courage and stepped between the boy and his mother. The mother watched her intently.

The boy retreated a little and cocked his arm toward Vicki, telling her to 'shut-up.' She held up a blood red, walnut-sized stone. "This is a carnelian agate. They're very rare."

The boy lowered his arm, staring at the stone.

"I've been hunting for rocks in a stream near here. I found some really special ones. Come and see."

He took a few steps closer. Vicki knelt on the ground beside her bucket, showing him the colorful contents.

He dropped his ordinance as the anger and fear melted out of his posture. He knelt beside her and began examining her treasure. He correctly identified several stones. "That's an agate. This is a crystal." He added, "I have a piece of obsidian at home."

They chatted about rocks for a while. Vicki told him how crystals can receive radio signals and other rock lore. She confided how rock hounding helped her to feel better when she was having a hard time.

The mother came nearer. Vicki heard her telling the person on the phone. "A woman is talking to him and showing him some rocks. I think it's going to be alright."

"Are you feeling better now?" Vicki asked the boy. He nodded his head.

Vicki let the boy choose a few stones to keep. He was soon quietly buckled into his car.
"Thank you," his mother mouthed.

Vicki mused on the experience. "I'm so glad that instead of casting judgement, or throwing emotional stones, I had the courage to offer kindness and understanding instead."

Only in America, God bless it.

Beth M Stephenson

Chapter 3   Love Is In the Air

Valentine's Day is always a happy day for American grade school children. "Room mothers" will provide millions of pink and white cupcakes and treats. Children will prepare special repositories for the exchange of Valentines.

When I was a little girl, it was a rare valentine that contained a little candy heart. The little paper cutouts carried heart felt messages like 'Be Mine' and 'Cool kid.' I doubt that I was the only one of my classmates to choose carefully for certain handsome, 8-year-olds.

One year, I had a huge crush on a certain Jamie Merigan. It didn't bother me that my best friend, Suzanne Pfister felt the same way about him. It started on Valentine's Day. We passed the usual cheap little cards to our classmates, but I inserted double the chalky conversation hearts into Jamie's flimsy envelope. I had to tape it closed so it wouldn't fall apart.

Apparently, Suzanne did the same thing, because the next day, Jamie told us that he had two girlfriends. The love notes began to fly, slipped into the lift-top desks, flung at each other as we ran past on the playground. Sometimes Suzanne and I resorted to chasing the boys (very literally) and when we caught them, we'd pin them down and kiss them. Jamie wasn't a very fast runner. Mr. Schindler's whole class knew about our classroom romance. Suzanne and I worked harder and harder to make better and better Valentines, well into March.

Then one day, Mr. Schindler decided that the crushes had gone too far. He placed a moratorium on passing love notes.

I was always an obedient little person and I never would have defied my teacher. But Suzanne was not so impressed. She made yet another card, decorated with a bride on either side of a likeness of smiling Jamie. The characters on the card were clearly identified. Word balloons floated like Hindenburg's above each head declaring, "I love you." She was a loyal friend, but she didn't tell me about the card until she'd already delivered it to our Beloved.

Jamie went straight to Mr. Schindler and gave him the card. Mr. Schindler posted the card on the bulletin board. When I came in from recess and saw the card posted in plain sight for the class to laugh at, I blushed to the tips of my toes. Jamie himself pointed it out to the rest of the class.

Now, I suspect that it wasn't true love. All my amour turned to an eternal hatred for that Jamie who betrayed us. I don't think I ever spoke to him again, even after he apologized. Suzanne went right on crushing on him, so it probably worked out for the best. Love triangles are never a good idea.

I received my first roses on Valentine's Day from my future husband. The day was definitely redeemed.

St. Valentine's Day has its roots long before America was conceived. It's thought to be a mix of an ancient Roman fertility festival and the Catholic commemoration of St. Valentine who was martyred for performing illegal marriages. In the 1700's the tradition of exchanging romantic and usually anonymous cards developed in England.

But Americans applied practical free enterprise and were the first to mass produce Valentine cards in the mid nineteenth century.

So this year, our American mass produced missives will adorn the decorated shoeboxes of children all over the country. Regardless of the way you celebrate it, I hope it's happy.

Only in America, God Bless it.

Chapter 4   Shooting Hoops

What's as American as baseball, hotdogs, apple pie and well, basketball?

March Madness is almost upon us, and some folks go a little crazy as the college teams battle it out over one of America's sport.

When I attended a college basketball game recently, the fanfare of a trumpeting band, earsplitting music on the public address, flashing and swirling spotlights, worked the students into a body of raucous, cheering fans. I had to smile as the crowd carried on basketball traditions, never written but handed down, one season after another. And all that was before the players even appeared on the court!

American basketball grew into a multi-billion dollar industry over the last century. I have to remind myself (and sometimes my overenthusiastic husband) that it's just a game. In the eternal scheme of things, it has (almost) no significance. Yet even with all my intellectual lecturing, I still find my stomach in knots, leaping from my seat for a well-timed three-pointer and generally behaving in a less-than-dignified manner.

James Naismith invented basketball in 1891 for the purpose of providing physical activities for young men in Springfield Massachusetts during the cold winter months. He wanted a game that didn't take too much space, so it could be played indoors.

The first 'baskets' from which 'basketball' takes its name were peach bushel baskets affixed to the balcony of an indoor gym. I suppose that kids these days are trained to shoot baskets early on, because those first years' scores were usually in the single digits.

That might have been a good thing, since when someone got the soccer ball to stick in the basket, the janitor had to get out a ladder and fish the ball out of the basket.

Before long, someone had the brilliant idea to cut a tiny hole in the bottom of the basket so the ball could be poked out with a stick. Before too long, they just cut the bottom out of the basket. In about 1906, the hoop, net and backboard were introduced.

At first, basketball was played and spread mostly through the YMCA. Before long, college sponsored teams were challenging YMCA teams in exhibition-type games. It quickly became popular and was deliberately introduced in nations around the world. By the time of World War I, it was beginning to be popular in other parts of the world and was widely popular in the USA.

The first rules established by Naismith called for 9 players on each team. Rules for passing were established as the man with the ball could not move. There was no such thing as dribbling.

The rule governing fouls read, "No shouldering, holding, pushing, tripping or striking in any way the person of an opponent shall be allowed. The first infringement of this rule by any person shall count as a foul. The second shall disqualify him until the next goal is made, or if there was evident intent to injure the person, for the whole of the game, no substitute."

Once a player got three fouls, he was disqualified. Three team fouls counted as a basket.

The three point line was first tested in 1940, and rejected. Two decades later, the American Basketball Association introduced it as a gimmick intended to make the game more enjoyable for the fans. It wasn't until the mid-1980s that it became widely accepted in every level of play.

Now, most kids have access to a basketball hoop, whether it's nailed to the front of the garage, affixed to a pole in a nearby park or in a community gym. Fans all over the country are pondering their brackets and planning their mid-March schedules around televised basketball games. I remind myself (and anyone else who needs it) that it's all in good fun.

Only in America, God bless it.

Beth M Stephenson

Chapter 5   New Orleans

The Revolutionary War didn't solve all of the newly formed United States foreign relations problems. By the time Thomas Jefferson received the reins of the nation, France and Spain were quarrelling over lands they controlled in what is now Louisiana.

The issue was access to the aortic artery to the heart of the land: the mighty Mississippi: namely New Orleans.

Jefferson recognized that the low-lying French city was critical to the national interests. France had already demonstrated a willingness to flex the gatekeeper's muscles. Some US factions were ready to go to war or even separate from the Union over New Orleans.

Jefferson commissioned his friend and protégé, future president James Monroe to join Ambassador Robert Livingston in France to make an offer on the valuable real estate. He authorized him to spend $10 million to buy New Orleans and get the 'Florida's' thrown in for good measure if they could.

What Thomas Jefferson didn't know was that Napoleon Bonaparte was already preparing to post a 'for sale' sign on all the French holdings in America. The territory had already shown itself to be unruly and cumbersome to govern. Besides that, he was planning a costly war with France's perpetual nemesis, England.

Monroe and Livingston never got to make their offer. Instead, they were presented with a proposal for France to sell the USA 828 square miles of land that included not only the coasts and city of New Orleans but part of modern Louisiana and Texas, all of Arkansas, Oklahoma, Missouri, Kansas, Iowa, Nebraska, South Dakota and parts of Minnesota, North Dakota,

Montana, and Wyoming. It even included parts of modern day Saskatchewan and Alberta Canada. The US paid $11 million plus cancellation of the equivalent of $4 million in debt. That works out to a little less than three cents per acre.

So New Orleans was worth $10 million and the other 800 square miles of land were worth $5 million.

Who can blame New Orleans if their ego is a little inflated?

The touristy French Quarter of New Orleans didn't seem to get the memo that they were incorporated into the US a while back. Picturesque flower baskets hang from elaborate iron work balconies. The hipped roofs and deep porches of typical French architecture abound. Street names are all French. The smells of Cajun cooking entice tourists into quaint eateries and street entertainers range from talented saxophone players to energetic boys with smashed aluminum cans transforming their athletic shoes into tap shoes.

Every year for Mardi Gras, (Fat Tuesday) the City erupts in an orgy of partying and parading that would make most saints blush. The holiday celebrates the beginning of Lent when Catholics fast and relinquish their besetting sins in hope of permanent reformation.

Hurricane Katrina drew all eyes to the fact that New Orleans is built on land that is below sea level. The dykes that keep the sea and the Mississippi River at bay were part of the original construction of the city. George Washington Cable wrote a short story called "Belles Demoiselles Plantation in the late nineteenth century. The story ends with the breaking of a dyke and the plantation being swept away in the flood.

Because of the high water table even in non-flood times, the dead are entombed above ground. The cemeteries resemble miniature cities of stone and are a popular tourist attraction.

It's easy to find excellent Cajun cooking but the can't-miss dining experience in my book is Café du Monde. They serve only little pillows of heaven called beignets (pronounced benyays,) and coffee or other traditional breakfast drinks. Beignets are hot donuts drenched in powdered sugar.

Whether you go for the music, the food, the culture or the history, New Orleans, (often shortened to 'Nawlins') adds a generous pinch of spice to the national melting pot.

Only in America, God Bless it.

Beth M Stephenson

Chapter 6   An American Patchwork Quilt

Have you ever thought of taking a history lesson from your bedcovers? While it may seem unlikely, the fabric of our nation has been preserved in the ubiquitous craft and art form of quilting.

When my friend Pam George died suddenly, our friend and avid quilter, Amy Anderson, gathered some of Pam's clothing to make quilts for her grieving children.

Amy's concept of remaking used clothing into quilts goes back to the practical needs of our first settlers. The old saying, "Use it up, wear it out, make it do or do without," suggests that throwing away the good parts of clothing with the worn out parts is simply wasteful.

Practical quilts are a way of preserving usefulness of worn blankets or clothing by stitching them together in layers to providing warmth.

Once Americans began to prosper, they also began to see quilting as an art form. They became more decorative than simply utilitarian.

Quilting bees became a common social event where women gathered to quilt each other's projects.

Both of the world wars had quilt-making as part of the war efforts, but mostly for auction to raise money for soldiers or the Red Cross.

When the Great Depression reversed earlier prosperity, many quilts reflected the downturn, reverting to being made of scraps of used clothing and leftover fabric. Their purpose returned to providing warmth more than decoration.

The art of quilting fell out of fashion in the 50's and early 60's, but the back to nature, eco-friendly and family history movement that started in the late 60's revived interest. Symbolic and traditional quilts have become more common since that time.

My daughter-in-law, Lindsay Stephenson, knew of my keen interest in American slave history. She made me a set of quilt blocks in patterns representative of a slave ship, an auction block, the Underground Railroad and a slave cabin.

The quilts from the area of Gee's Bend, Alabama are important to American folk art. The quilts are made by African-American quilters and their ancestors. They have a distinctly hand-made look, most often using primary colors.

The Anabaptists emigrated to Pennsylvania early in the 1700's. The Mennonites and Amish have developed distinct patterns and color schemes. The Amish quilts most often include a black background.

My friend Kathy Porter was the 2016 president of the Utah Quilt Guild. She recently showed me dozens of astonishingly intricate and beautiful 'art' quilts she had made. She demonstrated for me the process of 'paper piecing.' The tiny bits of fabric are sewn directly to the pattern in a designated order. Some pieces are barely a quarter inch and the process is so painstaking, it would cross the most patient person's eyes.

Kathy explained that art quilts are most often appliqued. Bits of colored fabric are glued in place like brush strokes of paint. When the design is finished, a felt or cotton filler and quilt back is applied by machine-stitching through the three layers. The quilting itself can add another dimension of pattern to the art work. This type of art is intended for vertical display.

Kathy admits that most people have a life and fit their quilting into scraps of time. She makes quilts and fits her life in between.

There are quilt guilds all over the country. The Utah Quilt Guild alone has over 1000 members and includes members from several neighboring states. The guild is divided into regional guilds which are further subdivided into 'bees' of 30-50 members that meet at least monthly.

There are many quilting techniques and hundreds of patterns within the techniques. Kathy showed me prize-winning art quilts, bed quilts, applique quilts, paper pieced quilts, and what she calls "fast" quilts. Her sewing and storage rooms are treasure troves of colors, patterns and quilting supplies. Her quilting machine dominates her basement family room.

With quilt guilds going strong all over the country, they promise to continue to preserve and to innovate this beautiful craft of American art.

Only in America, God Bless it.

Beth M Stephenson

Beth M Stephenson

Chapter 7   American Palaces

I remember seeing a catwalk in my friend's new house and being enthralled with the possibility of having something so interesting in a private home. It wasn't the modern design that I loved so much as the creativity and uniqueness of structure.

My Dad used to draw house plans in the winter and then build them in the summer months. But his houses were designed to be ultra-efficient, with the ultimate use of materials and time. His approach was mathematical, incorporating even the standard dimensions for plywood and drywall in the lengths of his walls. I eventually built one of his (modified) designs and it was indeed a lot of square footage for little cost. I added some false gables and a covered front porch to apologize for the efficient, rectangular box.

Though practicality outweighs my love of ornament when my own dollars are on the line, I love to tour the American palaces built by some of America's uber-rich.

In the middle of the 19th century, Cornelius Vanderbilt, a boy from a mixed race family of modest means left school at age 11 and began to follow his entrepreneurial inclinations. He became one of the wealthiest men in the world and his son, William Henry Vanderbilt doubled the family wealth.

Though Cornelius didn't engage in mansion building, William Henry and his grandsons made up for that. While Cornelius donated a million dollars to start Vanderbilt University, his sons built palaces on 5th Avenue in NYC and an astonishing summer home he named "The Breakers" in Newport, Rhode Island and Biltmore in Ashville, NC.

Built during the Gilded Age, Cornelius Vanderbilt II chose an Italian Renascence style for The Breakers, building the house

35

on a lot worth in today's dollars about $12 million. The home is distinct in my mind for including both family friendly touches and over-the-top opulence.

 The mansion that occupied the lot before The Breakers burned to the ground, so it is constructed of stone and as much fireproofing technology as existed before the turn of the 19th century was used in constructing the 70-room summer cottage. It overlooks the sea and is surrounded by magically landscaped gardens and a high wall with arched gates.

No Italian villa can top the views from The Breakers verandah, but the most distinct memory of touring that house-museum was the tale of how the children slid down the gilded staircase on mattresses, landing in the main floor ballroom. I used to do that as child and my kids did it too. Yet I don't believe that those uber-wealthy children enjoyed that activity any more on that golden staircase than we did on my uber-efficient, carpet covered stairs. The difference is that we used nylon sleeping bags and only did it when adults were not present.

About the same time as The Breakers was under construction by William Henry, little brother George Washington Vanderbilt, undertook construction of the largest privately owned home in the USA. The Biltmore in Ashville, NC is a vast estate covering more than eight square miles. The house itself has over 135,000 square feet of living space counting the basement swimming pool.

Rather than being a summer residence, Biltmore was designed to be entirely self-sufficient. GW Vanderbilt's idea was to raise all the wine, beer and food other than seafood on the estate and to generate its own electricity. Though not exactly a modern day prepper, with the help of the mild climate and fertile soil in that area, he very nearly accomplished that feat.

Biltmore is geared to more sedate and adult activities and entertainments with dozens of sitting rooms and elaborately carved libraries. Acres of themed gardens are filled with common and exotic species. Vast greenhouses supplied the house with fresh flowers, fruits and vegetables year round.

Though America must never have a king, we have watched the rise and fall of powerful families across the land. They leave a trail of fabulous architectural revels, house-museums, universities and lavish gardens. Most have been donated to the USA.

No, we don't have a king, but in the USA, if you can dream it, you can build it.

Only in America, God Bless it.

Jeff, Thomas, & Tricia at the Biltmore in Ashville, North Carolina

Walking the grounds at the Biltmore

Beth & Tricia at The Breakers in Newport, Rhode Island

Chapter 8   Hot Dam!

Herbert Hoover wasn't invited to the dedication of Hoover Dam. Franklin D. Roosevelt didn't even mention the former president whose name the dam would one day bear, in his speech. For its first eleven years, it was The Boulder Dam.

It was thirty years old by the first time I visited it. My cousins lived in nearby Boulder City, NV, and they still called it the Boulder Dam.

Of course we juveniles enjoyed all the dam jokes we could think of. But the most accurate pun used that day must have been 'hot dam!' The first summer of construction, the average high temperature was 119.

The Federal Government has built a bypass bridge so that through traffic over the dam is no longer possible, but when I first visited, US Route 93 ran right over the top of the dam. We parked in AZ and I leaned over the low wall. I'm not afraid of heights, I'm just afraid of falling off them. Gazing at the bottom 726 feet below, I instinctually pressed my horn-rimmed glasses tighter to my nose.

Inside, I was impressed by the beautiful art-deco adornments. Inlaid floors and other art inside the electric plant are now mostly off limits to the average 1 million annual tourists because of security concerns.

The Hoover Dam harnesses the Colorado River in The Black Canyon. The river marks the state line between Nevada and Arizona and the lake that resulted from the dam is called Lake Mead. It lies about thirty miles south east of Las Vegas.

Before the dam, Las Vegas boasted a population of just 6000, but once the project was announced, workers flooded into the region. Las Vegas even shut down its speakeasy's in the hope of housing the construction workers. But part of the construction contract was to build Boulder City to house the workers. In Depression wracked 1932, a project that employed over 5000 men was worth braving the hellish temperatures and sharing a bedroll with scorpions.

The Hoover Dam was the biggest in the world when it was built, but now ranks a puny 29th. 660 feet thick at its base and 45 feet thick at its top, it took 4.360 million cubic yards of concrete. It was poured in small sections that were artificially cooled. If the structure had been poured in one chunk, engineers estimate it would take 105 years before it was cooled, and would have begun to crumble long before that. As it is, recent tests show that it continues to harden even now.

But the arch-gravity style dam designed by John H Savage was only one piece of the massive project. Since the arch-gravity dam transmits the pressure of the water into the walls of the canyon above the dam, those walls had to be filled up with concrete, too. Millions of cubic yards of loose rock, soil and porous rock were hauled off of the canyon walls and lake bed that would become the sides and bottom of Lake Mead. After that, miles of bore holes were used to pump concrete into the natural rock to prevent seepage. The Hoover Dam is far more than a plug to create a lake. It is a complex hydro-electric plant that supplies power to residents as far away as Los Angeles.

Once the water pressure from the mammoth lake accelerates the water to 85 mph and it turns the 17 turbine generators, it is squirted out downstream to irrigate over a million acres of agriculture land in Arizona, and California.

112 people died in the construction of the dam, 19 from heat prostration. The average high temp the first summer of construction was 119. That doesn't count the 42 people that died from 'pneumonia' after working in tunnels heated to 142 degrees with gasoline powered equipment. Strangely, nobody in the surrounding communities died of pneumonia that year.

Built by a combination of 6 companies cleverly called 'Six Companies Inc.' it was finished two years ahead of schedule and dedicated Sept. 30, 1936. Hoover may have started it, but Roosevelt got the last word and it definitely wasn't 'Hoover.'

Only in America

God bless it!

Beth M Stephenson

Chapter 9   Harper's Ferry

The quiet little burg of Harpers Ferry lies at the confluence of the Potomac and Shenandoah Rivers. It's also where West Virginia meets Virginia and Maryland. I wanted to learn about John Brown. He was one ordinary citizen who shaped the course of the nation. I wanted to see the place where it happened and learn the details beyond the fact that his "body lies mouldering in the grave," as the Union soldiers used to sing.

Visitors park at the state parking lot and buy tickets to ride the shuttle into the historic district/museums of Harpers Ferry. It's like taking a bus ride back in time. The day we visited, it was melting hot and the cool waters of the Potomac enticed us to wade on the beach before we began museum hopping in earnest. We watched river rafters and canoers glide by on the Potomac with envy. Every now and then, roars from muskets rocked the air as antique firearms were demonstrated on the lawn near the river.

 When Thomas Jefferson stopped in Harpers Ferry on his way to Philadelphia in 1783, he stood on a rock above the Potomac and called the scene "perhaps one of the most stupendous scenes in nature." The comment points out how little he had seen of the lands that would become America.

George Washington chose the site for the national armory and arsenal in 1785. It was the weapon manufacturing plant and arsenal that was the target for John Brown's raid.

John Brown was a radical abolitionist. A tanner by trade, he had failed at several other business ventures. Fervently religious, he passionately hated slavery. He had twenty children. By many standards, he would seem like a crazy fellow, yet had he been successful in creating a slave uprising sufficient to overthrow the institution of slavery, hundreds of thousands of lives would likely have been spared in the Civil war.

Brown's intention was to seize the stockpile of guns and ammunition at Harper's Ferry and arm the slaves to overthrow slavery with each fighting in his local area. He had only 21 men, five of them were African Americans. But when accomplice Hayward Shepherd was mortally wounded, Brown called for the local doctor. When the doctor couldn't help Shepherd, Brown let him go. The doctor raised the alarm.

Lt. Robert E Lee was nearby on leave from the Federal army and was called to lead the forces to pin down Brown and squelch the uprising. Lt. J.E.B. Stuart was called to serve as aid-de-camp for the federal government. Ironically both men would soon be prominent leaders for the Confederate Army.

It was a short battle. Most of Brown's abolitionists were killed and Brown himself tried and convicted of treason against the Commonwealth of Virginia. He was hanged in nearby Charlestown.

The uprising was turned into a marching song for the Union Army. "Old John Brown's body lies a-mouldering in the grave," rallied troops to the cause. The lyrics of the song were a bit crass and irreverent, so Julia Ward Howe undertook to write "The Battle Hymn of the Republic," to use the marching tune and high concept without the vulgarity.

Captain John H. Hall had developed the use of interchangeable parts for firearms that were manufactured at Harpers Ferry. When the Federalists destroyed the town in 1861 to keep the Confederates from gaining access to the arms factory, it had already produced over 600,000 pistols, muskets and rifles. Confederates salvaged the machinery for making guns however, and moved it to the Confederate capital of Richmond, VA. Guns were never manufactured at Harpers Ferry again.

The air conditioning in the museums and historic buildings encouraged us to linger a little longer to learn about John Brown, the Civil War battle of Harpers Ferry where over twelve thousand federal troops surrendered, and the people that had given their lives in the struggle for freedom for all Americans.

Though John Brown's attack at Harpers Ferry seemed to fail, just a decade later one of the first schools to formally provide education for freed slaves was created there. Storer College operated there as a predominantly African American college from 1865 to 1955.

Harper's Ferry is still a beautiful place with inspiring history, a stepping stone in our path to equal rights and the cause of freedom.

Only in America, God Bless it.

Visiting Harper's Ferry with son Daniel's family

Above Harper's Ferry at Jefferson's Rock. Thomas Jefferson once stood here looking down towards the town. The Appalachian Trail also runs right by here.

Climbing the steep steps to the church in Harpers Ferry

Chapter 10   Super Mom

One of my heroes is my friend, Lillian Godwin. I first met her when we lived in Colorado and she moved into our church family with her husband Brian and four sons.

One of the first things I noticed about Lillian was that she was an attentive and loving mom to her boys. I soon saw that she was also friendly and compassionate. But it took a little while before I realized how deep her compassion and familial love ran.

Lillian always understood my jokes about 'testosterone poisoning' when describing the rough-housing among my own six boys or their delight in ruffling their sister Tricia's feathers. Lillian and Brian had always wanted a daughter, too.

I learned that before I knew her, they had saved the tremendous sum necessary to adopt a little girl from an Asian country. After paying the fee, the young company they had worked with went out of business and couldn't refund half their money. Their wallets were flattened and there were holes in their hearts.

A little while after I met the Godwins, several members of our church family adopted children through the Colorado State foster-adopt program. One of the adoptive mothers met two little Asian girls that had been placed in an emergency foster home. She knew Lillian's story and called her.

Lillian called the foster mother and learned as much as the foster parent could legally tell her about the two children. The four and a half-year-old had been terribly neglected, starved and abused. The younger child was in much better shape. Lillian went to meet the little girls. "The moment I saw them, I knew they were going to be my daughters," she explained.

It took several months to complete the foster-adopt parent paperwork. During that time, Lillian and Brian began giving respite care to the children so that they could get to know each other.

When they had successfully spooled through the red tape, they brought the children home for keeps. They changed their names by calling them by the combined old name and new name and gradually dropping the old name. Luckily, the names they had were similar to the family names their new parents wanted for them.

The law required a grace period to give the natural parents opportunity to retrieve their children. In Suzy and Emmalee's case, the abuse had been so serious that the waiting time served only to allow the children to transition emotionally from one family to another.

When the adoption was finalized and the girls were thriving, the Godwins believed their family was complete. Lillian loved all the trimmings and trappings of raising little girls and carefully eased the little ones through the traumatic adjustments, calling on all the support and help offered by state social services.

But then one day, their social worker called. The birth mother was pregnant. Multiple factors made it impossible that she could keep the baby, who was a full sister to Suzy and Emmalee. If Lillian heaved a weary sigh at the thought of another newborn at age 42, I never saw any hesitation. All of her friends gathered for a baby shower when beautiful little Camille came into the Godwin family.

I attended Cami's final adoption at the courthouse. The parents took an oath to care for her and raise her as their own, almost like a marriage. Nobody objected and the papers were signed. We celebrated with oversized hamburgers and milkshakes.

Lillian told the social worker to seal their file.

But two years later, the social worker called again. Suzy, Emmalee and Cami had a baby brother, born prematurely. The mother had been on the street and had not known she was pregnant. After she delivered the little fellow, she agreed to a tubal libation.

Lillian and Brian visited the biological half-brother to her daughters. He was so tiny, so needy, they couldn't resist. They had experienced the multiplication of their love with all seven of the older children and they knew that it would multiply again for baby Seth.

It hasn't been easy. Ordinary struggles children experience seem to be amplified by early stress. Lillian has battled through bouts of depression.

Seth is now almost 16. The younger four Godwins all show exceptional creative and artistic abilities. Lillian is unabashedly proud of all of her big, loving family. I'm unabashedly proud to be their friend.

Only in America, God Bless it.

Beth M Stephenson

Chapter 11   Americans in China Diversity

I recently visited Beijing, China. I soon noticed that we Americans were creating a much bigger stir than I would expect for such a well-behaved group. We felt like celebrities.

The few tourists from other European countries were generally ignored. What puzzled me further was that our American tour group included people from several different races, even including native born Chinese.

Our guide, who used the American name of Nina, was a native Chinese who had been a high school English teacher before she became a tour guide. Her daughter is about to graduate from Emory University in Atlanta and she has made extended visits to the US.

I asked Nina how the Chinese tourists could tell we were Americans. At first, she didn't understand the question. It was so obvious, she wasn't sure she understood. Then she answered, "In China, we love Americans. We love everything American. Your hair is a different color, your eyes are different colors, and you look different. We know your accent."

But almost half our group were Hispanic Americans and sometimes reverted into Spanish. When I pointed that out, she said, "It's true that in America, you come from all over the world. You're a mix of all different people from all over the world. But it's the way you are. You are happy. It's the way you walk and look. We can tell which people are from America."

I wanted to identify the difference.

Our clothing was the most obvious. Though many of the Chinese wear American brand clothing, I saw only one who wore short sleeves when all of our group had on short sleeves.

It was in the high 70's and all the natives had on overcoats, jackets or sweaters covering their arms. But I know that other Europeans wear short sleeves or sleeveless shirts.

After a few hours of observation, I concluded that the most distinct difference was our demeanor. As I watched my fellow American travelers, I recognized that our sense of freedom, openness and the expectation to be treated justly was somehow visible in the way we walk and speak and hold our heads. There was also a notable difference in the level of interest and enjoyment that the Americans seemed to express as compared with other non-Chinese tourists. Americans smile, point, and oooh and aaahh. European tourists were much less expressive.

One way or another, they certainly did recognize Americans.

While we stood on Tiananmen Square, a vast open pavement at the very heart of Beijing, a group of young Chinese women approached us. "May I speak to you?" one of them asked.

"Of course. What do you want to talk about?"

She asked where we were from and wanted to know why we had come to China. We told her we were tourists. She asked what sites we were going to see. Then she explained that she's an English major and doesn't have many opportunities to speak with Americans. She speaks American English, not British English. "I want to see how well I can speak with Americans." She thanked us warmly and turned away, almost giddy with excitement.

Nina said that English is mandatory in every school grade level.

Later, in the Forbidden City, we noticed that the young adult tourists were taking selfies aimed to include some of our group. Photobombing may be considered gauche in the USA, but it's apparently a favor when Americans do it in China. Twice, parents openly arranged their young children between us to pose for a picture.

It seems that we Americans are as unaware of our culture of freedom as the blood in our veins. It spans race, region and religion. But those who live with little freedom recognize in us what they lack. From what our guide explained, they have little understanding of what it means to live free. They imitate the brands we wear but don't recognize the roots that sprout our open, eager confidence and expectation of opportunity. But I am grateful.

Only in America, God Bless it.

At Tiananmen Square, Beijing (above) & on the Great Wall (below)

Beth M Stephenson

Chapter 12   Lighting the Way

I have always had a fascination with lighthouses. It may stem from being out on my dad's ocean fishing boat as the fog settled in on the Monterey Bay. The harbor mouth, already hard to identify from the water, quickly became obscured. I learned in an instant how critically important lighthouses are to seafaring folks.

Lighthouses are not an American invention. In fact, even our first American lighthouses were built while we were still the Cinderella to Great Britain. The east coast was already dotted with lighthouses by the time we flung off British rule and took off on our own.

One of the first orders of business after the revolution was won was to build a lighthouse at Cape Hatteras North Carolina. The shoals off the coast of the Outer Banks are treacherous because the warm Gulf Stream ocean current and the cold, northern Labrador Current, crash into each other, creating powerful ocean storms and unruly swells. The violent currents shift and wash sandbars, reshaping the ocean floor unpredictably. The only sure way to avoid shipwreck is to avoid the area altogether.

Lighthouses are not for the purpose of marking a specific pile of rocks or a sand bar. They are navigational landmarks used in conjunction with charts and navigation tools. Each lighthouse is identified by the interval of its beam flashes at night and its paint pattern and physical appearance during the day.

Since the earliest days of the United States, lighthouses have been controlled, built and maintained by the Federal Government. Lighthouses serve for the safety of the shipping and transportation industries as well as adding huge charm to a seaside landscape.

The Cape Hatteras Light house is known for its licorice candy diagonal stripes. It is essentially the third lighthouse structure to stand in that vicinity, with the earlier versions falling prey to the shifting shoreline and other weather factors. The first structure was considered deficient and was destroyed during the Civil war. The current structure was built just after the Civil War. It was moved about 2900 feet inland to escape the encroaching surf in 1999. Moving the structure was one of the boldest feats of civil engineering ever undertaken. It is the tallest lighthouse in the country at 198.5 feet tall and it weighs about 5000 tons.

Far inland on the shores of Lake Superior on Green Bay, similar water conditions create dangerous currents and unpredictable shoals. In fact, Door County Wisconsin got its name from the strait at the tip of the peninsula and Chamber's Island. There were so many shipwrecks in the area that the strait was known as Death's Door. There are eleven lighthouses in Door County, and many of them were built around the time of the Civil War.

Most of the Door County lighthouses are incorporated into the keepers' dwelling. When I visited the Eagle Bluff lighthouse in Peninsula State Park on the east side of Green bay, I found that though all of the Great Lakes are fresh water, the maritime flavors of the place feel as authentic as any of its salty cousins. Operated now as a museum, it is a quick time travel into 19th century life with all of its pleasures and complexities explained.

 For many years, water for household use was carried up from the lake. In 1882, when the lighthouse was 14 years old, the lard-burning lantern was replaced with a kerosene burner. For years after that, the fuel was stored in the base of the tower which was part of the family living area.

 When the second keeper was in residence, The Eagle Bluff light served to guide ships through the channel between the low-lying Strawberry Islands. The whole region of Door

County, WI reminds me of Nantucket/Cape Cod, MA, 1000 miles to the east.

Both of these lighthouses are equipped with valuable Fresnel lenses. Developed to concentrate the light like a traditional convex lens but with much less mass and volume, the lens is ridged to provide powerful magnification, casting their beams twenty miles in fair weather.

Lighthouses are part of the history and charm of hundreds of American coastal regions, and even on our freshwater inland seas.

Only in America, God Bless it.

Door County, Wisconsin lighthouse from the water (above) & from Peninsula State Park (below).

Chapter 13   A Place Americans must not Forget

The corn would have been eye high by early July. The peaches were nearly full size. But the peaceful town of Gettysburg was a crossroads in the center of a caldron that was about to boil over.

General Robert E Lee of the Confederate States of America had decided that his loyalties lay first with Virginia. His beautiful 1100 acre estate lay across the Potomac from Washington DC in Arlington, Virginia. It was overtaken the day after Virginia seceded. The Union pointedly began burying their war dead surrounding his house as punishment for forsaking the Union.

Ostensibly, the war was about states' rights. But the issue was the spread of slavery. Though Lincoln is credited with guiding the torn nation in the interest of freedom, his own writing suggests that he would preserve the union at all costs. He expected slavery to die out because it was morally wrong.

Lincoln had fired an ineffective general and replaced him with George Meade. The Union had information that Lee's army was concentrating near Gettysburg, PA for another assault on the North.

The Union army got there first, claiming the better position on the hills to the north of town. It was a sweltering July 1. Most men wore wool jackets over their shirts. Townspeople scurried for cover.

By July 3, the battle boiled south of town with the union on the high ground of Big Round Top, Cemetery Ridge and Little Round Top.

In town, a young woman named Ginny Wade was kneading bread dough when a stray bullet hit her, killing her instantly. She was the only woman to die in the battle of Gettysburg. Her fiancé, Jack Skelly was a corporal in the Union Army who died of his injuries before learning that his sweetheart was already dead.

General Lee made a crucial mistake by ordering Lt. General James Longstreet to attack the union army who held the high ground. Maj Gen George Pickett was ordered to take the center position, opposite Cemetery Ridge. The assault included a long charge over open fields in the scorching heat.

The Confederates were driven back and defeated, but not until 50,000 American lives on both sides of the battle had been sacrificed. It still stands as the costliest battle for American lives in history.

Right triumphed. The Battle of Gettysburg marked the beginning of the end for the Confederate States of America and their effort to protect slavery.

Now millions of tourists visit the battle ground each year. There were plenty of heroes in the 1863 battle and now there are multitudes of monuments. The visitor center boasts an elaborate reenactment walk-through diorama (and wonderfully cool air conditioning).

In November of 1863, President Abraham Lincoln visited Gettysburg. Renowned for getting to the point he offered one of the shortest and most revered speeches in history.

"Four score and seven years ago our fathers brought forth on this continent a new nation, conceived in Liberty, and dedicated to the proposition that all men are created equal.

Now we are engaged in a great civil war, testing whether that nation, or any nation so conceived and so dedicated, can long endure. We are met on a great battle-field of that war. We have come to dedicate a portion of that field, as a final resting place for those who here gave their lives that that nation might live. It is altogether fitting and proper that we should do this.

But, in a larger sense, we cannot dedicate—we cannot consecrate—we cannot hallow—this ground. The brave men, living and dead, who struggled here, have consecrated it, far above our poor power to add or detract. The world will little note, nor long remember what we say here, but it can never forget what they did here. It is for us the living, rather, to be dedicated here to the unfinished work which they who fought here have thus far so nobly advanced. It is rather for us to be here dedicated to the great task remaining before us—that from these honored dead we take increased devotion to that cause for which they gave the last full measure of devotion— that we here highly resolve that these dead shall not have died in vain—that this nation, under God, shall have a new birth of freedom—and that government of the people, by the people, for the people, shall not perish from the earth."

Only in America, God bless it.

Granddaughter Kate near the monument to the 20th Maine (lead by Joshua Chamberlain) on Little Round Top, Gettysburg

Field where George Pickett lead his ill-fated charge. This is the view from the Union lines.

Son Daniel & granddaughter Kate at the battlefield

Chapter 14   American Hospitality

It seems to be an oft repeated theme in American history. Out of the darkest hours come the greatest deeds of compassion and heroism.

It was 1839. Missouri Governor Lilburn W. Boggs had issued executive order #44, otherwise known as the Mormon Extermination Order authorizing Missourians to "exterminate or drive Mormons from the state." It was rescinded in 1976 with an apology by Missouri Governor Christopher Bond.

The Mormon town of Far West Missouri was ransacked and burned. Women were raped, and some men had been killed. The leaders of The Church of Jesus Christ of Latter-day Saints had been imprisoned in a jail, ironically named "Liberty."

The issue was more than religious intolerance. Mormons were largely northerners with strong abolitionist sympathies. Missouri had entered the Union as a slave state less than two decades earlier. Tension increased as Mormons immigrated to the state. Missourians feared political power would shift to abolitionists if Mormon communities continued to grow.

The result was that 5000 Mormons were driven from their homes and threatened with death if they didn't leave the state. The winter of 1839 was brutally cold. The destitute Mormons arrived at the Mississippi river just west of the tiny community of Quincy, Illinois.

The citizens of Quincy were horrified by what had been done to the refugees. As a free state, leaning strongly toward the Whig (later Republican) party, they were already certain of their moral superiority to their slave-holding neighbors across the Mississippi. But politics aside, their compassion was nothing short of heroic.

Though a town of just 1500 citizens in January of 1839, they marshalled their citizens into a relief brigade. The Quincy Whig wrote on March 3 1839, "The Mormons—We hasten to invite the attention of the charitable and humane, to the destitute condition of some of this people. A large number of families are encamped on the opposite bank of the Mississippi, waiting for an opportunity to cross, who are, we understand, almost without common necessities of life. Having been robbed of their all in most instances, by their merciless oppressors in Missouri, they have been compelled to hurry out of the state. . . . If they have been thrown upon our shores destitute, through the oppressive people of Missouri, common humanity must oblige us to aid and relieve them all in our power."

The citizens of Quincy crowded the refugees into the shelter of their homes. They fed and clothed them and helped them to find work.

It must have been a long, meager winter for both the givers and receivers in Quincy. The Mormon leaders were released from jail late in April and quickly made their way to Quincy. Joseph Smith, president of the church, urged the Mormons to prepare to depart from the homes of their generous hosts as soon as possible. They were to begin draining the swampland he had bought for the building of a new town 45 miles north of Quincy.

Less than a decade later, the Mormon city of Nauvoo flourished and was the largest in the state of Illinois. Fear of Mormon political clout caused them to be driven out again. This time, they moved far to the desert west where they built Salt Lake City.

More than 165 years had passed when the tables were turned. In 2006, the Mississippi River was in flood stage and towns up and down river were flooding. The town of Quincy was threatened by rising water and the failure of upstream levies.

The Mormons remembered the debt owed to the town of Quincy and they responded with particular eagerness. The Church of Jesus Christ of Latter-day Saints gathered a force of 130 missionaries and members in that region to form a sandbag brigade. They worked shoulder to shoulder with the citizens of Quincy to shore up the restraints on the floodwaters. Quincy was protected.

Kindness, compassion sacrifice and generosity changed the course of history long ago, but the effect of those Americans' goodness ripples through our nation still today.

Only in America, God Bless it.

Wagon with oxen at Nauvoo

Beth M Stephenson

Chapter 15   Ouachita Lake is a Gem

My son-in-law, Walt, told us to bring our snorkeling gear and our kayaks. He was bringing his water skiing boat and his dad was bringing the little sailboat. It seemed strange for a tent camping trip, but we took him at his word. He'd been to Ouachita Lake (pronounced Wah-shi-tah) in the center of Arkansas before.

I was a little surprised to find such a well-developed tourist site in a place I'd never heard of. Our first glimpses of the lake through the pines and hardwoods was remarkable for the intense blue shade I associate with the crystal waters of tropical seas. The hot, moist afternoon doubled the lure of an evening swim.

I admit I'm not too finicky about swimming in natural waters. My rules are simple: It has to smell clean and not have chunks of ice or trash floating in it.

But even the princesses that prefer a chlorinated swimming pool to a spectacularly beautiful natural swimming hole could have no complaint about Lake Ouachita's lovely water. Walt told us to bring our snorkeling gear because swimmers can easily see the fish, freshwater mussels and even a rare form of freshwater, (non-stinging) jellyfish.

We set up our tents sprawling several campsites. It wasn't exactly campfire weather, but I had a new(ish) Dutch oven and I had premixed a hot fudge pudding cake. Walt had his Dutch oven cherry cobbler ingredients ready to go, too. We could skip the fire, but we needed 48 hot coals to bake the desserts.

I posture myself as a responsible adult for staying in camp to help get the meal ready in the pressing heat while a cool swim in the luscious lake lured me away.

Lake Ouachita was originally built in the 40's and 50's for the purpose of flood control and the hydro-electric energy produced by the Blakely Mountain Dam. One little town had to be moved to high ground before the dam was finished in the 1950's. Though the Blakely Mountain Dam was originally proposed by a power company, when financing became an issue, the Army corps of engineers took over the project. The dam is built of earthen fill from the area of the lake bed.

The engineers   probably didn't anticipate how perfectly clear the waters of the lake would be. Nor did they likely anticipate that the 40,000 acres of lake surface and 975 miles of shoreline would one day support posh marinas, hundreds of islands and extensive water-sport/fishing tourism. As we paddled through one of the marinas in our lowly kayaks we ogled the floating mansion houseboats stored under the covered dock.

Jeff and I kayaked a couple of miles along the lakeshore the next morning. Though we were staying in a campground the shoreline seemed as pristine as any high mountain lake. We enjoyed the fish and hawks and even a stray turtle. We beached our boats and swam in a private little cove. It was quite romantic for a couple of old codgers.

 Later, my son, Scott and I took Walt's little Sunfish to the far shore and back for some pleasant sailing. The water was almost flat then, but later, the wind came up and tried to obliterate our camp. Walt told us of camping on that point when he was a Boy Scout and their staked tents were uprooted and blown into the lake.

It was the end of the season when we visited, but an evening swim in the designated area was an absolute must, especially with our tummies full of chili dogs and hot desserts. The tents had warmed to the unbearable level and without wet hair, Frog togs towels on our chests and no rainfly, it would have been impossible to sleep. Walt's Dad, (Walt) even tried unsuccessfully sleeping on the top of a picnic table to escape the heat.

Ouachita Lake is an Arkansas state park with everything from glamping to houseboating , water skiing to kayaking, tent, cabin and RV camping sites. It is one of the cleanest lakes in the nation and with beautiful surrounding scenery. With Hot Springs National Park and other nearby lakes, it's part of the Diamond Lakes area. It is certainly another lovely American gem.

Only in America, God Bless it.

Beth M Stephenson

Chapter 16   The Melting Pot

Have you ever heard of Hobo Stew? It's a dish where many folks bring some sort of savory canned or dry food and then combine it in a big pot. The results are never the same twice but I've never had it that I didn't enjoy it. There's always something out of the ordinary that a jokester dumps in, but that gives the flavors and textures interest. It's an easy menu for camping trips and youth activities.

It seems to me that Hobo Stew is a much more apt description of our American culture than "Melting Pot." The term 'melting pot' renders thoughts of pots of bubbly cheese or rich chocolate and not diverse and interesting textures and flavors or unexpected treats.

I don't call myself a foodie, but I'm always willing to try something new when I run across it. (I did draw the line at the little road side stand selling barbequed rats in Thailand). The funny thing is that as I've travelled the world, almost without exception, I like the Americanized version of international foods better than the original.

The French gave us the Statue of Liberty and French pastries. That's the only instance in my experience where we truly can't improve on their national specialty.

I first noticed this phenomenon when I ordered tacos in Mexico. The corn tortilla was raw! Where was the sour cream, the melty cheese, the guacamole? It turns out that to a Mexican, a taco is a corn tortilla that enfolds meat. If it enfolds beans, it's a burrito. Truthfully, the common Latin America meal uses the tortilla as a vessel to carry beans and rice to the mouth. All the rich flavors and preparations are mostly a north-of-the-border creation.

I was eager to try pizza in Italy. Oh what one of our Papa pizza makers could teach the Italians about pizza! The most common and preferred pizza in Italy is the Margherita style. It's the three colors of the Italian flag, green from basil, red from tomato sauce and white from (water buffalo) mozzarella. I ordered it one day along the Amalfi coast and it was bread, a huge slice of wonderfully flavorful tomato with slightly melted cheese over it. Italians usually buy it by the slice and fold it into a calzone.

If it sounds boring, well, it is boring in a yummy sort of way. It didn't catch on in the USA because it was nasty. We took a good thing and made it better by piling on the savory meats, vegetables and even pineapple. Different cities claim rights to different style of crusts, toppings, and sizes. St. Louis even has its own style of cheese.

The Chinese food I ate in Beijing tasted suspiciously like an American Chinese restaurant. Our guide explained that the menus are developed to appeal to tourists. "If you want chicken feet and other foods you have never seen, you have to go away from the place where visitors come." Even as it was, there were some dishes that were extremely unappetizing.

I've had Pad Thai in Thailand. Theirs is very simple and tasty. Ours is not-so-simple and fantastic. They eat bugs in Thailand. There are somethings left well-enough alone.

Of course Americans didn't invent smoking meat, American barbeque is a messy romp through gastronomical Wonderland. The heated competition between barbeque styles rages between cities and even states across the south. Memphis and Charleston closely guard their dry rub recipe for smoked pork parts. Kansas City brags about its sauce and Texas declares itself the king of brisket. Oklahoma City is the crossroad where you can find the best of everything.

Apple strudel came from Germany and became American apple pie. Our version is sweeter, wetter and more 'appley'. We took German sausages and smoothed out the texture and gave them a cuter name. German braunsweiger would be denied entrance to the stadium while 'hotdog' hits it out of the park.

Our American Hobo Stew is not only a changing blend of cultures, customs and beliefs it is also an innovative and ever-changing menu as we blend different flavors from all over the Earth.

Only in America, God Bless it.

Best French Toast I've ever had, at The Attic in Long Beach. It had Chantilly Cream & a carmelized topping.

Yummy pizza at The Wild Tomato in Door County, Wisconsin

Beth M Stephenson

Chapter 17 A Day to Remember

Memorial Day is much more than the unofficial start of summer. It's much more than the date fashionistas give permission to begin wearing summer white. It's more than a day to throw a barbeque and party hearty.

Memorial Day was started the year after the end of the Civil War and called 'Decoration Day.' It called for a day to "strew with flowers" the graves of the soldiers that had given their lives in the recent war. The bodies of the dead were buried in almost every village and town across the country and the wounded nation needed to honor those who had not been spared the ultimate sacrifice.

It was held in the spring because that was when the War Between the States had ended and in the month of May because there was no particular battle that matched that timing. The southern states first honored Decoration Day at different times, mourning not only the dead soldiers but the loss of the war.

The Civil war cost more in American lives than any other conflict in US history to date. It required the establishment of National Cemeteries. The Union began burying their war dead on Confederate General Robert E Lee's estate directly across from Washington DC at Arlington immediately surrounding his house as a way of salting the earth so that he could never live there again. After General Lee's death, the Supreme Court determined that the estate had been illegally seized and ordered its return to the family in its original condition. Rather than exhuming the bodies of fallen soldiers, Lee's son sold the property to the Federal Government for $150,000. Lee's mansion still stands in the midst of our honored dead.

Now there are bodies of fallen soldiers from every war from the Revolution to the Gulf War interred at Arlington. During the Civil War, the bodies of 5000 unidentified soldiers were interred there. In 1921, the US built the Tomb of the Unknown Soldier and interred the remains of a fallen WW I soldier. Nearby unidentified bodies have been interred in the immediate guarded area.

The tradition of adding a fallen unknown soldier ended with the Vietnam War when DNA testing successfully identified the remains interred as an unknown soldier. His body was removed from the tomb and reinterred with honors at a national cemetery closer to his home.

I remember accompanying my grandmother to a cemetery on Decoration Day when I was a young child. The cemetery smelled like a lavish garden, with new-mown grass and a kaleidoscope of flowers covering the graves. I remember that my grandmother wanted to go first thing in the morning to be first to place her blooming tribute on the graves of loved ones lost. I remember that every single grave had some decoration on it by the time we finished and not just fallen military.

So Memorial Day has become a day to remember those who went before. We fly the American flag and decorate our doorways with Red, White and Blue. For those who have lost close family members to the cause of freedom, the day is a day of remembering, a national Sabbath made holy by their willing sacrifices. Others will remember non-military loved ones lost and place some memorial on their graves.

I will remember not only those who gave their lives in battle, fighting for the principles that have provided the peace and prosperity that Americans currently enjoy, but also those who had the vision to prepare the way by laboring in their own fields of endeavor. They bettered themselves to one degree or another, but built a foundation upon which their posterity would thrive. Whether it's flowers or flags, it's a day to remember the human cost that provided what we enjoy.

Only in America, God Bless it.

Robert E Lee's home at Arlington National Cemetery

The Tomb of the Unknown Soldier at Arlington National Cemetery

Visiting Arlington National Cemetary

Chapter 18   Home Sweet Home

Americans don't live like most of the world. Our freedoms and opportunities have produced what we politely call a 'middle class.' But when measured in lifestyle, Americans live better than most of world's wealthy class.

Take Real Estate for example. More than 60% of Americans own their own home. Of homeowners nearly a third don't have a mortgage. Even among the lowest wage earners, (those households earning less than $31,000 per year, 35% own their home.

Land and the yen to own it has been the driving force behind much of our nation's growth and development, so it's no wonder that homeownership is often the first financial mile marker we reach for.

My husband and I had four kids before we bought our first home. We scraped and sacrificed, wringing every cent from our budget to save enough to buy a home. Jeff's parents agreed to lend us enough extra for a down payment to avoid paying (costly) mortgage insurance. With the money we saved by not paying mortgage insurance, we paid back the loan.

The real estate agent we contacted went out with us one day and showed us a series of dumps. Rusty car parts hidden in knee deep grass were the norm. But I was determined to have three bedrooms, two bathrooms in a safe neighborhood with a fenced yard. "It doesn't exist for that price," the agent said.

But we persisted and eventually found a promising classified ad. The glowing description read, '3+2, 1300sq ft $60 K auction, hardwood, carpet' with the address. We drove by and found tidy little homes with fenced back yards.

The house was trashed inside. A haze of smoke stung our virgin lungs. Pornographic posters hung on the bedroom wall.

Plywood showed through holes in the linoleum. The gold shag carpets were crisp. It was stinky from filth. The fixtures had been torn off the bathroom walls, leaving gaping holes in the drywall.

But there were indeed two bathrooms! Our offer of $59,000 won the auction. Lucky us.

I gave birth to our fourth child and we closed on the house the next day. We had two weeks to make the house livable before we had to move from our rental.

We were too poor to hire help, so in those two weeks we chipped out decaying floors, laid vinyl flooring, scrubbed and repainted every inch of the walls and ceilings, and cabinetry, patched drywall, sewed window coverings and replaced the fixtures. We killed the black widow spiders, roaches and mice.

The kids played in the jungle of a back yard and now and then I'd stop to nurse and cuddle my newborn. When Jeff got off work, he'd work late into the night laboring at the 'new house.'

We lived in that house for a year and a half and never stopped working on it. We got the overgrowth in the yard under control, finished replacing the second bathroom floor, took down the mirror tiles, and learned a huge repertoire of skills. By the time we sold it to accommodate Jeff's job transfer, we made back 300% of the money we had into it.

We bought another fixer upper but it wasn't nearly as bad as the first one. We only had to put in a yard, lay new flooring and strip decaying wallpaper. We were coming up in the world.

Eventually Jeff let me apply all my mad house skills to building a house as an "owner builder". The project turned out well and when we transferred from the construction loan to a permanent mortgage, we started with $80,000 in new equity. After we sold that home 12 years later, we were able to pay cash from then on.

When Jeff retired, we meant to buy down. But we found a fixer-upper for a great price and now live in the biggest home we've ever owned. Now we have YouTube to teach us new skills. We just couldn't resist triggering another round of American prosperity.

If we can do it, anyone can do it.

Only in America, God bless it.

The happy couple at home

Beth M Stephenson

Chapter 19   Just Keep Swimming

Tis the season of watersports and air conditioning, icy drinks and ice cream cones. It's also the season of teaching the tadpoles to swim.

I remember the exciting smell of chlorine and rubber bathing caps beckoning me to hurry into my swim suit at the high school swimming pool. The rubber flowers on my cap flapped gracelessly as the foggy morning breeze nipped my snowy skin.

Nowadays, kids have a huge variety of 'camp' opportunities during the summer months and the tradition of swimming lessons is not as ironclad as it once was. In fact, even in my children's generation, I rationalized my way out of swimming lessons. They learned to keep themselves afloat and doggie paddle, but they never had formal lessons.

So when my middle son Daniel applied for a job at a boarding school for troubled boys, he had to admit that he was not a skillful swimmer. He was 6'3" tall, however, built like Mr. Clean and just as bald. The fact that he was applying to grad schools to be a psychologist was probably secondary to his muscles in landing him the job.

Part of the rehabilitation for the boys was to train for a triathlon. The coach laughingly told him that he would soon be a competent swimmer. Every day, he would spend at least an hour in the pool, swimming with the students. Biking and running also helped get him into the best condition of his life. But most importantly for this story is the fact that he became an excellent swimmer.

Fast forward four years. Daniel has completed his doctoral program and when he finishes a one year internship, he'll be a licensed Psychologist.

He's also a husband and a father. Last weekend, he was picnicking at Cheat Lake near Morgantown, WV with his family. They were splashing and playing on the sandy beach as they watched a group of young adults swim out far beyond the designated swimming area. Suddenly, they heard one of the young men calling for help and splashing around.

Daniel and Lindsay stopped playing and watched, thinking for a moment that the kid was joking. One of his companions swam over to help but after a brief struggle, the friends separated with the one still calling for help.

Daniel charged into the water and quickly went into triathlon mode. By the time he reached the drowning swimmer, the boy had sunk below the surface. Daniel pulled him up and placed the drowning young man's hands around his neck. Though not an ideal lifesaving technique, his strength and stamina enabled him to bring the boy back to shore alive.

"I was really tired," Daniel admitted.

The young man sat on the shore quietly for a while. He explained to Daniel that he had a heart condition and his stamina had given out. Daniel didn't think to ask his name.

As his mother, I tremble to think of the alternative outcomes to my son's act of heroism. How many mothers have grieved for their sons or daughters who gave their life for their fellow Americans.

But somewhere in West Virginia, there's a family that is NOT in mourning. There's a young man with his whole life still ahead of him. I'm grateful that I don't have to pay the consequences of deciding that swimming lessons were too inconvenient or too expensive.

I'm proud of my son but I know that as an American, he grew up thinking in terms of community spirit and watching out for others. It's part of our national culture. Equal rights translates into equal concern for others.

So heroes are fine, but they're not uncommon. Every town, every neighborhood has their share. Perhaps their deeds are not usually so dramatic, but everyone caring for others as well as we can helps make America great,

Only in America, God bless it.

Grandkids at Cheat Lake, near Morgantown, West Virginia

Beth M Stephenson

Grandson Andy at the beach

Chapter 20   Crazy Bet and the Hero Mrs. Bowser

We've just celebrated Juneteenth again! It's fun to remember the black freedom fighters that turned US history.

Elizabeth Van Lew deserved to be called "Crazy Bet." She went around Richmond, VA at the height of the Civil war muttering to herself. Though a wealthy heiress, she dressed in ragged clothes and often offended her high-society associates with her odor.

Yes, she deserved her title. But Elizabeth wasn't crazy. As a staunch abolitionist, she was a shrewd spy, operating a spy ring to help the union army. Her deliberately cultivated 'crazy' nickname helped her operate unnoticed in the shadows.

Her most effective spy was a black woman who had been a slave in her father's household. Mary Elizabeth Bowser was highly intelligent and beloved by the family. When Elizabeth Van Lew's father died, she freed Mary and all their slaves and freed Mary's family members, too.

Mary remained in the Van Lew household as a paid employee and friend. She had been formally educated in the same Quaker school as Elizabeth. So she knew the customs and demeanor of a respected and valued friend and the subservient invisibility of a house servant.

Mary Bowser agreed to go undercover into the Confederate White House as a house servant to Jefferson Davis. If she was caught spying, she would be killed without the trouble of a trial.

Taking a page from the methods of her mistress, 'Crazy Bet', she presented herself as a dimwitted but competent worker, possibly using the alias, Ellen Bond.

It was illegal for slaves to be taught to read or write, so her abilities had to be carefully hidden. She pretended to be too dull to understand the strategies and military reports discussed as she cleared the table or poured the coffee.

Mary had been a slave, serving as a house maid. She would have been trained to be invisible. But their 'invisibility' lulled their masters into the idea that submissive behavior stopped their servant's ears from listening and minds from remembering. Ironically, the Davis's must also have assumed that their servants had no interest in the struggle for their own freedom that raged across the nation.

Jefferson Davis and his confederates probably never even noticed her presence while they discussed surprise attacks and troop movements. Letters and plans were left lying in the open where Mary had easy access. She was a fast reader and had an excellent memory.

Daily she silently collected information and then passed it to another of Crazy Bet's ring, a lowly baker. Nobody noticed him either as he made his daily deliveries and spoke briefly with the servants.

Sometimes Mary hung the laundry in view of the street in a coded pattern. An upside shirt beside a blue shirt and then a white one might mean that certain troops were headed south in the following week and were short of ammunition.

Her secret acting career lasted almost two years. Though Jefferson Davis wrote to others that he knew there was a leak in the mansion, he never thought to pay attention to the slow-witted servant. But Mary Elizabeth Bowser and her husband fled the Confederate mansion shortly before the south surrendered. Nothing is known of what became of her or why she fled when she did.

Mary Elizabeth Bowser's records were destroyed by the US government with all the other Union spies' records for their own postwar protection. Her legacy has been reconstructed from private letters and Elizabeth Van Lew's diary.

But wherever her grave, and whatever the alias that protected her, Mary Elizabeth Bowser was a woman whose courage, talent and moral convictions leave America in her debt. As certainly as any freedom fighter, we honor her,

Only in America, God Bless it.

Elizabeth Van Lew (above) & Mary Bowser (below)

Beth M Stephenson

Chapter 21   In Which Type of Barn Were You Born?

Everywhere I travel in the USA, I'm on the lookout for interesting barns. Perhaps on some subconscious level a well-kept barn translates into a well filled table and my stomach is closest to my heart.

Riding along in the Pennsylvania countryside, red and white barns contrast with the vibrant green grass like a Christmas card. Some are blazoned with advertising like "Drink Milk" or "Eat Beef." I imagine that inside, the floors are kept clean by automatic flushing systems. Dairy cows are milked with shiny, sterile machines and the milk never has contact with air until it's poured over my oatmeal.

In the Great Smoky Mountains of Tennessee, unpainted crib barns have stood sturdy and functional for more than a century. The upper floor, used for storing feed, overhangs the lower animal pens or shelters. The cantilevered roof provided a sheltered spot to disembark from a wagon or buggy and a spot of shade in the relentless summer heat.

In the south, tobacco barns fling wide their doors to let air pass through for drying the tobacco leaves. Ventilation is the first consideration when constructing that sort of structure.

For a time in the 19th century, round barns became all the rage. Thoughtful farmers realized that round barns are geometrically efficient because they create a high wall-to-area ratio. You get a lot of space for little cost with a round barn. But it's easier to build a square or a rectangle, so though they are quaint, the style is uncommon today.

The most typical barn style is the western barn. It's a large rectangle with a gambrel roof. The roof is relatively flat toward the top, giving lots of headroom in the hayloft on the second floor. The second part of the roof slopes very steeply, often nearly coming to the ground.

When I was a young girl, a family friend invited us to spend Easter on his family farm in Southern Utah. The Saturday before, their teenage son took us out to the barn to show us the moon on the cows udder. It was a very special cow, a sight not to be missed.

The barn was English style, a rectangle with a gabled roof. As with most English barns, it was unpainted. The double doors swung out and our host led the cow into a milking stall. He hobbled the animal so she couldn't kick and instructed us (one at a time, to get our faces right down near the udder so we could get a good look. Then he squirted us with a jet of warm milk. His side splitting laughter suggested that he was unaware that the joke had been played on 'city kids' (we raised apples and no livestock), for generations immemorial.

Bank barns are built into a hillside so that the basement and the middle floor are both accessible from ground level. Potato barns are buried up to their rooflines to keep the interiors cool.

My kids were delighted to find a rope swing that dropped them into a pile of straw in a barn in central California.

A trained eye can tell what is produced on a farm by looking only at the style of barn. In the west, massive Dutch barns with square footprints and simple gabled roofs are needed to store feed for large cattle herds. Dairy country in Wisconsin and California need spacious structures to shelter the animals themselves and to process the milk.

Prairie barns have a door on the gabled end with stalls on one side of an aisle and feed storage on the other side. The central area was historically used as a threshing floor. Hay and straw were stored in the loft overhead. (Hay is food, straw is bedding).

So whether a Prairie or a Crib, an English, Dutch , Round or Bank barn, they embody the richness of the land,

Only in America, God Bless it.

Barn at a cherry farm in Door County, Wisconsin

Round Barn at Arcadia, Oklahoma, on Route 66.

Beth M Stephenson

Chapter 22   Our Flag Traditions

The United States of America is a young nation. Yet we have traditions designed to promote the values and principles we uphold. Though a youthful nation, these customs have already helped to inculcate American values into each generation.

On Independence Day, I lined the walkway leading to my front door with small, inexpensive flags. I made certain that whichever way the wind blew that day, the little banners would not brush the ground.

Later, as we watched a parade from our lawn chairs, we rose to our feet and placed our hands over our hearts as the national banner passes by. It's automatic to me after pledging my allegiance throughout my school days, yet I feel a swell of patriotic love and gratitude when I do it.

The Pledge of Allegiance doesn't go back as far in our history as the governing principles it espouses. The Pledge was written by a socialist, Francis Bellamy. His intent was that the pledge would work for any nation in the world. It was first published in 1892 in *The Youth's Companion.* His version read, "I pledge allegiance to the flag and to the republic for which it stands, one nation, indivisible with liberty and justice for all.

The idea that all the world would be governed by republics and desire liberty and justice for all was lofty indeed. But since oppression and injustice are the order of most of the world, the pledge never caught on.

The salute to the flag was also performed differently at first. A uniformed military member was to salute with the palm facing down held beside the right eyebrow. When the words "the flag" were stated, he was to extend his arm with the hand rigid toward the flag and hold it in that position while finishing the salute. Non uniformed citizens were to place the hand over the heart and similarly point to the flag when mentioned.

As the rumble of World War I approached, the words "to the United States of America" were added.

The salute was further altered when Germans adopted the "heil Hitler" salute that seemed similar to our flat-palmed-arm extended salute. Public policy was changed to keep the hand over the heart or at the brow throughout the salute to make the distinction.

In 1954, as America's religious ideals were threatened by cold war Communism, President Eisenhower asked Congress to add the words, "under God" to the pledge. This fluid development of the pledge distinguishes American values as other nations around the world deviate from the principles of freedom, personal liberty and equal representation and protection for all Americans.

"I pledge allegiance to the flag of the United States of America and to the republic for which it stands, one nation under God, indivisible with liberty and justice for all.

Similar traditions promote values in the proper folding of the American flag. Just as the flag itself has symbolism embedded in its various elements, the folding of the flag reinforces those symbols.

The flag is folded lengthwise with the stripes folded over the top of the starry, blue field. The flag is then folded again with the starry field encasing the end of the flag. The striped end is folded once so the corner meets the folded edge in a triangular fold. Each triangular fold has national and religious symbolism.

Such things as mortal life, eternal life, honor of mothers and fathers, Jesus Christ, the God of Abraham, Isaac and Jacob, the honor and fidelity to our nation are represented by each fold of the flag. Finally, the red of honored dead and the purity of our quest for freedom for all represented by the stripes are enfolded in the starry heavens as mortality is encompassed in the heavens.

When the flag is unfurled at dawn, and the red and white emerge from the night, it symbolizes the resurrection of the dead.

We honor our flag by protecting it from touching the ground as we protect our nation from taint of unworthy objectives and the dishonor of defeat.

President George W Bush met with emigrant Lopez Lomong before the 2008 Olympics as Lomong prepared to bear our nations colors in the Olympic procession. The president reminded the athlete not to let the flag touch the ground. After the ceremony, Lomong reported that his hands ached from holding the flag so tightly.

We are defined by our traditions. Our traditions are an expression of our values.

Only in America, God Bless it.

This flag covered the coffin of Jeff's dad, who was a World War II Veteran

Beth M Stephenson

Chapter 23   America's First Home

The thought of putting on a wool coat in the middle of the summer with humidity high and temperatures higher was enough to raise a rash all by itself. The windows were the only source of ventilation and they were all locked shut. Every breath was air that had been breathed 100 times already.

But the meeting was secret. No hostile eavesdropper could linger outside the Pennsylvania State house and get information about the goings on inside.

Gathered inside were representatives from all the American states except for Rhode Island. Their mission was to reform the Articles of Confederation to better serve commerce between the states. The men gathered were leaders and men of strong opinions. Among them were several that loved the sound of their own voice and assumed that the assembly enjoyed it as much.

But even with all the heated opinions and the interior misery in the breathless room, the men began to form a consensus. What America needed wasn't a mere reformation of the Articles of Confederation. They needed a brand new style of government. They needed to blend the principles of democracy with the mechanics of a republic.

Three different branches of government must each provide counterbalance to the other two. It would be a stable government. Just as a three-legged stool is always stable, the branches would share equally in promoting and supporting the national well-being without being able to seize too much control.

The new constitution was written and re-written. It had to be perfect. How many times in the history of the world had men gathered for such a purpose? Personal ambition, or a yen for power or authority was to be thwarted by the voice of a self-governing people. They built the structure to last forever, like a Roman arch with freedom as the keystone.

This wasn't the first gathering of world changing importance held in the Pennsylvania State House. More than a decade earlier, some of the very same men had gathered to codify the separation from British oppression. They created a document declaring themselves independent from British rule.

That meeting, though not as secret as the later Constitutional Convention, was also held in the height of the summer heat. Debate raged. Thomas Jefferson wrote and rewrote the document. The original Declaration of Independence written by Jefferson, outlawed slavery, declaring all men created equal regardless of race. That clause threatened to dissolve the potential unity of the colonies with Southern colonies refusing to endorse it if that clause was left in. Jefferson, a slave holder himself, fatefully removed the clause.

Almost 100 years later, the building where the Declaration of Independence and the US Constitution had been debated and ultimately signed, held the body of Abraham Lincoln in state on its way back to Illinois for interment. The clause had been returned at the cost of over 600,000 American lives.

The Pennsylvania State house was eventually renamed Independence Hall. It has an open lower meeting room and more open areas and offices on the upper floor. A magnificent clock tower was part of the original structure and has been replaced over the years to be like the original.

The building is 107 feet long and 44 feet wide. The first floor where the action happened has a central hall with the 1520 square foot gathering room where the conventions were held on the east side of the building and an almost identically sized courtroom on the west side.

The first time we tried to tour Independence Hall, we learned that there were no tickets available, regardless of the fact that we were there in plenty of time. It's regulated by the number of tourists and not the time of the day.

The second time I went to see it, we got our tickets online in advance and had no problem.

People speak in hushed voices and treat the hall with due reverence as the birthplace of freedom, with justice and liberty for all.

Only in America, God Bless it!

Independence Hall in Philadelphia.

Beth M Stephenson

Chapter 24   The Queen Mary

She's an English lady, an expat retired to the shores of Long Beach, California. Hitler put a bounty of $250K on her for any ship's captain that could sink her. But she could outrun a torpedo and was just too fast to catch.

She is the Queen Mary. Launched in 1936 she had a glamourous and swashbuckling career as a Brit. Over 1000 feet long and 118 feet wide, she was double the size of the Titanic but built for speed. Her purpose was to deliver the mail from Southhampton England to New York City in under a week. The passage usually took her 4 or 5 days.

She was built for speedy mail transportation, but she was competing with other ocean liners for passengers. So the walls were painstakingly adorned with magnificent woodwork and the grand public rooms were decorated to please the rich, the famous and the royal.

Her exterior was repainted battleship gray during WW2 and the Queen Mary served as a troop transport ship. She still holds the record for most people onboard a ship at sixteen thousand. She was nicknamed the 'Gray Ghost' because nobody could find her.

Journals of soldiers carried to Europe aboard the Queen Mary speak of debilitating seasickness and relentless rocking. The stabilizing technology that keeps modern cruise ships from pitching or rocking too much had not been invented when the QM was launched. Ship's logs show that she rocked as much as 20 degrees. The onboard menu for troops was not fancy. Tomato soup and crackers for dinner and oatmeal porridge for breakfast rarely had a chance to be digested anyway.

300 people were injured when she met her first storm, because hallway handrails hadn't yet been installed.

Now the beautiful ship is permanently moored in Long Beach, California. Retired as an ocean liner in 1967 when she became too expensive to operate and with air transportation becoming common, the city of Long Beach bought her. They paid 3.5 million and spent over 120 million preparing her for life as an American.

Now permanently moored in Rainbow Harbor, she's still afloat but disabled by the removal of her boilers. Though she'll never traverse the Atlantic again, she serves as a posh hotel, an event center, tourist attraction and museum. Unlike a modern cruise ship, the ocean liner whispers 'old money.' No expense was spared in making her spectacular in her 1930's art deco costume.

The top deck Sir Winstons boasts some of the finest dining on the west coast. Though pricey, it's a romantic destination restaurant with views of the harbor and the Long Beach skyline. The Beef Wellington I ate there was some of the most wonderful food I've had in my mouth.

The rooms have been updated in amenities without diminishing the feeling of a 1930's ship. The portlights (the correct name for a porthole) are left open day and night to catch the fresh sea breeze. The beds are comfortable and everything is scrupulously clean. It feels very much like a step back into time.

The interior of the ship is in wonderful condition but the exterior of the ship is in serious need of paint and other repairs. Long Beach has allotted 23 million for Queen Mary's immediate care and plans to spend five times more than that all together in repairs and enhancements.

Her original decks are teak wood held in place with pegs. The grand ball room feels like a step back in time when the music is about to start and Katherine Hepburn is at one table and Winston Churchill is at another. Photos of superstars and royalty taken on board the Queen Mary are scattered throughout the ship. One museum currently has a collection of

English royalty artifacts and Lady Diana's wardrobe and other keepsakes. The other is a display related to The Titanic.

The Queen Mary is the last of the ocean liners. She's protected by an American city that loves her. I'm so glad to have the chance to see and feel and experience that era through the Queen Mary.

Only in America, God Bless it.

The Queen Mary in Long Beach Harbor

One of the Queen Mary's lounges

In the dining room with the Commodore

On the way to eat at Sir Winston's

Chapter 25   Gators in the Glades

We pressed our noses to the windows of our ancient RV as the south Florida landscape flattened. We knew we were entering alligator country and I was as eager as any of my children to see my first alligator in the wild. Oh what glee when I saw one in a roadside ditch! And then another. And another and another. Soon, they were like a patterned wallpaper.

Though much of south Florida is covered with terrain that is part of the Everglades, only a portion of the region is actually part of the Everglades National Park. We'd been driving for an hour in country that looked like the Everglades but were still miles from the official boundary.

At last the RV bumped into an unpaved parking area. We were there for an airboat ride. The water was low that year, and the day was scorching. As we waited for the tour to get ready, we visited some penned animals and stared stupidly at grasshoppers big enough to swallow a small poodle.

Our pilot handed us each two cotton balls as we boarded the small craft. We were instructed to stuff them in our ears. Airboats are built to traverse extremely shallow water. Rather than a propeller in the water which would instantly be tangled with grass, they sport a giant fan on the back of the boat. They're called airboats, not because they float on air, but because they use air pressure rather than water to propel themselves.

They sound similar to a medium sized jet engine. We certainly didn't have to worry about taking any animal by surprise.

Once underway, the pilot ushered us to one ecosystem after another. A hammock is a pocket of deeper water where earth berms support trees and shrubs. We saw baby alligators, barely two feet long and grandfather alligators. The creatures were used to the airboats. When the drivers stopped the boats, they'd gather nearby, hoping for a treat from the driver's pocketful of marshmallows. It turns out that those big, wicked-looking teeth include at least one sweet tooth! We also saw bird's nests and even some endangered species.

On to the River of Grass ecosystem that surrounds the hammocks. The airboat skimmed over the low grassy plains. Suddenly, he killed the engine and invited anyone who wanted to, to climb out of the boat and go for a little wade.

I was horrified when my oldest son hopped up and stepped out of the boat. "Alligators don't come into these parts," he blithely told me.

Rob's bravery encouraged several other passengers to try it, too. Despite my protectiveness of my son, he was in his late teens and if he was eaten by an alligator, it seemed like natural selection. Who was I to argue with the laws of nature? He neither got bitten by an Everglades monster, nor sucked into the mud. He said the bottom was more sandy than muddy. I contented myself by accepting that I was a coward.

There are many different ecosystems in the Everglades region. Large mammals like deer or panthers haunt the piney islands. Mosquitoes the size of humming birds descend in clouds like something out of an Alfred Hitchcock movie on tourists who were too cheap to buy the repellant.

At the tip of the park, rare crocodiles coexist with their reptilian cousins and flamingos decorate the shore. The day we visited, one of the kids found a pink feather but no flamingo attached.

Though a vast and complex system, the Florida Everglades are also fragile. Though this year has seen much higher water than in recent years, the fluctuations in weather can quickly cause jeopardy for the flora and fauna of the region. Exotic species, introduced by man either deliberately or accidentally also create competition for the food supply. Species like the boa constrictor are non-native and pose a threat to the eco system because they tend to thrive and then crowd out the natives.

But regardless of the season, the Everglades thoroughly deliver American alligator viewing and enough adventure to keep mothers trembling. If you go, get the strongest mosquito repellant you can find and then bathe in it. Reapply each time your skin melts off in the heat.

Only in America, God Bless it!

Viewing the gators from the safety of the airboat.

My kids (Chris, Thomas, Brian & Tricia) at Everglades National Park.

Chapter 26   Long Beach is Reborn

We were definitely the country cousins when we went to visit my Uncle Bob and Aunt Eleanor in Long Beach, CA. My cousin Ray is close to my age and as we swam in the canal alongside their yacht moored behind their house, it seemed like he had a childhood charmed like no other.

But on our way to the elite island section of town called Naples, we would drive through the Long Beach down town. It was a puzzling paradox, with rundown street fronts and dusty shops. In the 60's, there was nothing glamorous about Long Beach.

But the city administrators eventually took matters in hand. They reviewed their assets. A terrific harbor, mild, sunny weather, residential neighborhoods for the uber-rich on Naples Island, and a very, very long beach. Easy access to Disney Land, Hollywood and other LA area attractions didn't hurt either.

Americans are risk takers and Long Beach undertook a pull-up-by-the-bootstraps reinvention into a world class tourist destination. It was a tremendous financial risk. But the alternative was unacceptable.

They started by acquiring the retired ocean liner, The Queen Mary. A tourist city needs tourist attractions. Thousands of US troops had crossed the ocean on her sumptuous decks on their way to and from the European theater during WW2. Long Beach repatriated her into a nautical hotel with posh restaurants, rentable event areas and interesting museums.

The Pike amusement park had deteriorated into a dangerous area with bums and prostitutes. There was no saving it. The site was razed and then reborn into a pleasant walking/biking/ skating marina roadway with polished retailers and a wide variety of mid-priced restaurants. The bridge that links Rainbow harbor walkway to the outdoor mall area is reminiscent of the old roller coaster and a Ferris Wheel still gives the beachy/Pike feel.

The Acquarium of the Pacific is nestled adjacent to the Pike area. Hundreds of school age children swarmed it the day we visited, but the Behind-the-Scenes tour geared to adults fascinated us. Stingray and shark touch and feeding areas are memory makers. Sea robins, puffer fish, sea dragons compete for attention with sea otters, seals and sea lions.

City Planners soon turned their attention to their natural assets. A classmate of my cousin Ray's, Michael O'Toole started a gondola ride business called Gondola Getaway. Jeff and I were alone in our boat with our gondolier, Eric Sjoberg. He regaled us with local history, advised us of the tradition of kissing under each of the 5 bridges and then serenaded us with Italian love songs in a rich baritone. The boats are authentic Venetian gondolas.

The stately old buildings have been renovated into trendy beach condos. New hotels overlook the palm-laced marina and tourist shops in Shoreline Village. The anchor business in Shoreline village is Parker's Lighthouse restaurant with waterside dining and excellent sea food.

The long beach itself is protected by a long breakwater so the surf is never high enough to facilitate surfing, but at the back of the beach, there is one path paved with springy rubberized pavement for joggers and walkers and another path for cyclists/skaters. The bike share system that dots the city allows people to pick up a bike in one part and drop it off at any other of 50 stations. It costs just $21 for 4 hours of total ride time.

At Rainbow harbor, there are reasonably priced harbor cruises, whale watching trips and Catalina excursions. We saw hundreds of dolphin, some sea lions and a magnificent blue whale on our whale watching trip.

In the center of the downtown there's a long shady walkway. Shops, restaurants and parks line a pretty street where no motorized vehicles are allowed.

Long Beach has assumed the title of the aquatic capitol of the world. With Olympic level athletes in beach volleyball, swimming, rowing, water polo and lots of other sports and water-related activities are abundant and readily available.

The Long Beach transformation is nearly finished. Polished streets, an abundance of murals and inlaid art sidewalks in the downtown make the city fun to walk. Some of the city bus routes are free and frequent and the rest are low priced. Exceptionally good restaurants of every ethnic variety should attract foodies. (The Attic for breakfast, George's Greek Café for lunch and Sir Winston's on the Queen Mary for dinner were my three favorites.) There's plenty of room on the beach so that it's never crowded. The sun shines 350 days a year and the locals are welcoming and helpful. The Long Beach airport is nearby and extremely simple to navigate.

Their risk has paid off. Long Beach is fresh and clean and fun, having successfully replaced their other faltering industries with tourism.

Only in America, God bless it.

On our sunset gondola ride in Naples

Shoreline Village near downtown Long Beach.

Chapter 27   Million Dollar Highway

I am a brave woman, one tough cookie when it comes to adventure. No princess complex here. But I have one fear, terrible and debilitating. I'm afraid of winding mountain roads built on the shoulders of tall cliffs. The type I mean don't have guardrails. I firmly believe they don't have guardrails because it's far too dangerous to install them on the brink of an abyss.

Yet on the other hand, I love spectacular scenery. My heart sings when I look out over a mountain vista, blue mountains layered into the distance or lacy waterfalls plunging into a riot of foam. What is lovelier than a mountain meadow bedecked in wildflowers?

I didn't investigate when my beloved husband planned a southern Colorado camping trip and said we were going to traverse the Million Dollar Highway. "It's supposed to be extremely scenic," he mentioned casually. "It's on the list of America's most scenic byways."

That sounded right up my alley. He knew my terrible fear and it never crossed my mind that he was setting me up for an hour of sheer terror.

The Million Dollar Highway got its name supposedly because it cost a million dollars per mile when it was built in the 1880's. Its purpose was to carry silver ore from Silverton to Ouray. Other folktales claim that the road got its name because of the million dollars worth of gold in the rock excavated to make the highway.

We were driving our Ford Clubwagon that seated 12 people that sunny day. It had nearly 200K miles by that time and the steering was getting a little loose. We had already been enjoying a combination of camping and quaint motels, and that day was set aside for scenic sightseeing. Since Jeff usually drives while I ooh and ahh the scenery, it was my turn to drive.

I drove south from Ouray, Colorado on Highway 550. By the time we encountered our first hairpin turn, there was nowhere to turn around. The pavement gained altitude like a ski lift bunching itself to vault over Red Mountain Pass. The S curves seemed to follow the path of a giant sidewinding snake.

Did I mention that there are no guardrails? In fact, the lanes are so narrow that the white line that indicates the right side of the lane disappears where the road was too narrow to allow the width of a paintbrush.

There are other places where an outside curve chokes the protruding mountain so that the road appears to vanish into a rock face. There's nothing but blue sky visible through the windshield, and drivers must take it on faith that a Russian emigrant engineer named Otto Mears understood the difference between a road, a scenic overlook and a footpath.

Jeff began to exclaim over the astonishingly beautiful views. I told him sharply to 'Be quiet!'

The kids started making jokes about untimely deaths. "Hush!" was all I could say. I didn't want stronger language to be my last words.

It started raining. There was a little waterfall rolling across the road, its descent barely interrupted by the pavement. I had to peel two fingers off the steering wheel to turn on the windshield wipers.

 Instinct said to stop and call for a helicopter rescue. I have since read that drivers freeze up on that road every year.

 Did I mention the steering was loose?

If there was an entrepreneur with the courage to harness himself to the rock face about half way through that pass who offered to drive tourists to safety, he would be a millionaire in less than a year.

I didn't stop. There was no entrepreneur. If I had, the driver coming around the blind curve behind us would rear-end us, pushing us into the bottomless gorge. No, it was better to meet death bravely.

The speed limit on that 12 mile stretch is 15 mph. Jeff tells me that the scenery is some of the most majestic and awe-inspiring he's ever seen.

I wouldn't know.

Only in America, God bless it.

Beth M Stephenson

Chapter 28   That's An Old City

The Spanish built it. The English wouldn't arrive for two decades and the pilgrims would not see the rocky northern coast of Massachusetts for 55 years.

The Spanish were looking for a good place to build a fort from which to attack the French. King Philip II ordered Pedro Menendez de Aviles to go to the new land and help ensure they could protect their claim on North America, or at least the Florida region. After all, legend held that the Fountain of Youth was nearby.

Though the man, St. Augustine is a widely accepted Christian saint, the new city was not named for his concept of a utopian 'City of God.' The conquistadors sighted land on the north east coast of Florida on the Saint's Catholic feast day, August 28, 1565 and so it was named in his honor.

The July day we visited was melting hot. Jeff was eager to see the stone fort, the oldest remaining (non-indigenous) structure in European America, excepting on Puerto Rico. Our collection of sons were always up for cannons and dungeons and our daughter was interested in history, too.

The Castillo de San Marcos fort is provocatively medieval. That day, the Spanish flag drooped in the sultry air, stirring now and then as though aroused from sleep. We explored the living quarters, the batteries, and the dungeons. The kids enjoyed siting down the cannons at imaginary foes.

 I found myself craving ice water and musing on the thought of putting a wool jacket and trousers over my cotton clothing in the prickling heat. No wonder those early explorers were constantly attacking each other. Who wouldn't be irritable!?

Later we explored the Colonial area of town. It's even older than the fort and is replete with pirate flags, ships swimming through snow-globe storms, and embellished plastic sunglasses. A few of the old structures remain to suggest life in the era of foreign queens and kings struggling to build the bakery that would create the American pie. My thoughts seemed to recur to baking often that day.

In its earliest days, The native Saturiwa tribe was unimpressed by Spanish land claims and burned the first fort down. Later, Dominique de Gourgues a French soldier, led an attack on Spanish holdings. With the Saturiwa, <u>Tacatacuru</u>, and other Timucua peoples, they drove the Spanish to build the bigger, better stone fort if they hoped to control territory in America.

Once in a while, pirates attacked the fort just to fill a lull in international struggles for control. Sir Frances Drake attacked the spot and though a hero to the English, the Spanish called him a pirate. In the 1570's, his behavior helped the Spanish conclude that they needed to build a masonry fort that could not be burned down. But when pirate Robert Searle attacked in 1668, Spain got serious and funded the construction.

Designed by Ignacio Daza, as a masonry star shaped structure with a large, square courtyard in middle, it was also surrounded by a dry moat. What is more swashbuckling than a moat?

The Spanish eventually succumbed to the English who succumbed to the American Patriots who then lost control to the Confederate States and then regained control.

The existing Castillo de San Marcos has been remodeled and repaired over the years but was in constant military use until 1933 when the fort was decommissioned.

Forts aren't much use in our age of high tech weapons. But it makes a great tourist attraction and feels like treasure from our history.

A charming black and white lighthouse in the modern town of St. Augustine evokes thoughts of a giant licorice candy and tourists are the only marauders. The Spanish flag still flies over the fort, reminding us that they were first to begin adding ingredients to the melting pot that would become the USA.

Only in America, God bless it.

Son's Brian and Thomas on the ramparts of the Castillo de San Marcos

Son Chris posing by one of the fort's cannons.

Beth M Stephenson

Chapter 29   Furry, Feathered and Scaly Americans

I wanted to see a bald eagle. I had my camera lens cleaned and battery charged as we exited the cruise ship in Ketchikan AK. Before long, I spotted the impressive raptor on top of a totem pole. Tourists snapped pictures as the bird struck steely-eyed poses like a rock star. Before long, however, we realized that bald eagles are more common than crows.

I suppose every area of the US has its unique fauna. American Alligators are a dime a dozen in parts of Florida, Louisiana and Mississippi. Black bears in the Great Smoky Mountains quickly become passé.

Mule deer became a terrible pest in Colorado. We tried all the old-wives-tale remedies and found only one (strong scented soap hung on the lip-level branches) worked. At Christmas time when people bring out their fake, twinkle lit lawn deer, it's about the same to me as putting Christmas lights on a cockroach or other pest.

When we were moving from Colorado to Oklahoma, our realtor sent me a picture of some deer grazing in our soon-to-be back yard. She wrote, "I hope you have many more of these peaceful scenes in your new home." I wondered if we could back out of the contract to buy the house!

Our neighbors complain of rabbits eating their garden and squirrels chewing their patio furniture.

I saw my first live armadillo at Lake Fausse Pointe State Park in Louisiana. My kids were so excited that they chased the critter into the underbrush. It was lightening fast but that might have had something to do with the six boys chasing it.

A few years later, we suspected an armadillo was digging holes all over our back lawn. We set a critter trap and caught a fat, sassy armadillo. We knew that they can carry leprosy and were not keen to touch it. But how to dispose of it? I wanted to shoot it, but Jeff said that wasn't sporting. Since when am I a sportsman? He carried it into the woods and let it go. We had new holes the next day.

That same critter trap also captured a hissing, snarling raccoon, an irritable possum and two skunks. Skunks have a very effective way of teaching humans to stop setting critter traps. They have no respect for property rights or even sincere apologies.

It's hard not to be impressed when a heron or pelican spreads its wings to lift off from a leisurely lake shore.

We used to have a red fox that denned on our neighbor's lot in CO. Every spring, she'd be sitting proudly on her front stoop, with darling little fur balls playing around her. We always knew, however, when we had new neighbors when the posters went up on area light poles advertising a missing cat.

One morning, a great horned owl rousted us by hooting on our roof ridge.

We were enthralled when we met our first American Bison in Yellowstone but not so much when they stampeded around our car in South Dakota

The process of getting a green garden snake out of our window well recently was as entertaining as a circus clown act.

 Once when our son Chris peeked into a bird nest atop a downspout to check for eggs, he found a live massasauga rattle snake.

I encounter cottontail rabbits and a feral cat my grandkids have named Sniff on my daily walk. Jackrabbits and coyotes, and hawks haunt the field behind our back fence.

The quail we encountered on a recent hike looked all ready to go to the opera with their feathery headdresses.

Biologists estimate that 432 species of mammals, including sea mammals are indigenous to the US. Birders delight in more than 800 varieties of birds, Entomologists revel in over 100,000 known insect species. 295 sorts of amphibians, 311 types of reptiles and 1154 types of fish round out our American family.

Only in America, God Bless it!

Bighorn Sheep in Colorado

Manatee in Crystal River, Florida

Here's the fawn in our backyard

Chapter 30   Yippee Ki Yay for the Rodeo Cowboys and Cowgirls!

As I crouched in the rodeo stands with my camera pointed at the chute where a bull rider was about to emerge, a young man paused behind me, unwilling to photobomb my shot. When I turned back, satisfied with my efforts, I noticed the young'un.

There are very few Americans that don't look spiffy in a cowboy hat. Male or female, it seems to be the perfect shape to set off most features well. This particular fellow wore a simple cowboy hat. His smile showed perfect, white teeth and bright blue eyes. His western shirt and blue jeans seemed pretty authentic for a rodeo, but his boots were clean, unscuffed leather. No, he may have been magazine cover material, but he wasn't going into the arena on a bronco any time soon.

 The word 'rodeo' is Spanish for 'roundup'. The competitions no doubt sprung from the testosterone rush of a bunch of cowboys that had completed the grueling task of branding the calves in a herd of cattle.

Several places in the west claim to be the birthplace of modern rodeo, but the general consensus is that Prescott Arizona deserves the title. The event held there on July 4 1888 set the standard for organization, prizes awarded, rules for competition and even the events themselves. They were apparently the first folks to realize that people would pay admission to watch the super cowboys perform.

The event I attended recently wasn't my first rodeo. In the first, a gigantic bull found a gate insufficiently fastened and charged into the parking lot. There were no thumbs in the belt loops for the animal handlers as that ol' cuss led them on a merry chase around the pickup trucks and family station wagons. They had to stop the show for almost an hour while they tried to herd that critter back to civilization.

The air was rich with the scent of animal dung, funnel cakes and corn dogs.

The announcer informed the cheering crowd that bareback bronco riding was the most dangerous of all the rodeo events. It hardly seemed possible compared with bull riding. But as the cowboys launched out of the shoot, hats flying, hands waving crazy spirals in the sky and their spines jolting impossibly against the bucking, plunging, horses, I wondered how anyone could walk away from such a beating.

Nobody could stay on the bulls for the required 8 seconds so the prize money was unclaimed.

Mutton busting is the kiddie version of bronc riding. Some of the kindergarten-sized competitors clung like a tick on a dog, riding belly down with their cheek on the sheep's rump and legs around the sheep's neck. The sheep gathered quietly at the other end of the arena after they shook off the little parasites.

Barrel racing is a women's event where the horse and rider circle three barrels, either two to the right and one to the left or two left one right. In the US, speed is the only element of judging.

Between the typical events, trick rider Kyzser Stoddard rode his bridle-less Spice in every position other than sitting in the saddle. Spice had been slated for the glue factory with bad ankles and thought to have an untrainable disposition. Now she entertains with spunky grace, anticipating Kyzer's tricks without physical prompting.

I watched cowboys hang above the backs of half-ton animals as they nerved up to give the nod that they were ready for the gate to be opened. I could see fear in their faces, but rodeo breeds a special kind of courage. My stomach lurched every time the nod came.

One bronc cowboy injured his wrist and another limped badly, but nobody seemed too seriously hurt.

The announcer summed up rodeo. "When we get to the ticket window in the sky, it doesn't matter if we won or lost, it's how we made the ride."

Only in America, God Bless it.

Beth M Stephenson

Chapter 31   USS Yorktown

Dementia had taken hold of my Uncle Harold when I last visited him. He was still himself, commenting on my weight, (he could make a fence picket feel obese) and teasing me about whatever else about which I might be sensitive.

But then he lapsed into storytelling. Though many of his other memories had slipped away, he repeated stories from his WWII days as a pilot in the Pacific theater. He had wanted to be a commercial pilot until the war. But once it was over, he didn't fly again.

Harold explained the terror of landing on an aircraft carrier for the first time. "You had to get it perfect the very first time. There was no margin of error," he remembered.

He told of a time he was flying a bombing mission. As the planes got close to their target, they armed the bombs so that they were ready to drop. But when they arrived at their target, they couldn't see well enough to risk dropping their payload because of fog. Their only alternative was to turn around and scuttle the bombs into the open ocean. There was no way to disarm a bomb once it was ready to drop.

But one pilot forgot to scuttle his bombs. By the time the conning tower on the aircraft carrier saw that the bombs were still on the incoming plane, it was too late. The bombs exploded on contact, killing the pilot and a number of men on the deck.

I don't remember which aircraft carrier he flew from. But I remember visiting the USS Yorktown at Patriots Point Museum in the Charleston Harbor in South Carolina. Standing on the shore, it's hard to conceive of a structure as mammoth as the Yorktown floating, let alone clipping along at 33 knots. It routinely made the run between Pearl Harbor and San

Francisco in 4 days. The Yorktown fully loaded weighed 36,380 tons. It was 872 feet long, (think three football fields!) before being remodeled into an angled launch ship when it gained about 8 feet. It is about 50 yards wide.

The USS Yorktown has C-10 after her name to indicate that three earlier US ships also bore her name. All four were named to commemorate the Revolutionary war battle of Yorktown.

Touring the ship was more like touring a military base than anything mobile. There were multiple cafeterias, vast barracks with bunks stacked like storage bins and expansive below-deck hangars where not-in-use airplanes (and later, jets) were stored.

Other than the captain's quarters, there's nothing much cozy on an aircraft carrier, or any other military ship, for that matter. Painted metal in shades of white and gray are standard.

 Though the mammoth ship has become a museum piece, her military career spanned 40 years. The giant ship served as a mobile launch for crippling air strikes. Such a deadly advantage was an important enemy target. Consequently, she didn't stay in any one place for long. Her missions were intense and incisive, but then she would withdraw to safer waters.

Such tactics didn't always protect her. Though several direct attacks, including Japanese suicide missions were thwarted by her guns or over shot their target and landed in the water beyond her decks, one bomb found its target near the conning tower, penetrated the deck in the hangar deck and exploded, blowing a hole in her hull. Yet other than the loss of American life that resulted from the incident, the Yorktown continued on her mission, still fully operational.

The Yorktown was started just a few days before the bombing of Pearl Harbor and commissioned in 1943. She was later refitted as a submarine defending ship. She served in both

WWII and Vietnam and earned 11 battle stars. She even recovered the command module from the Apollo 8 moon mission.

With such a long career as an invincible ship, it's no wonder that she was chosen as the set for the movie about the Pearl Harbor Bombing, "Tora, Tora, Tora."

Now, decommissioned and disabled, the USS Yorktown is the star of the show at the Patriot's Point Museum. She is a national historic monument and serves to safeguard the memories of many Americans who lived and died in the defense of freedom.

Only in America, God Bless it.

The USS Yorktown at Patriots's Point, Charleston, South Carolina.

Onboard the USS Yorktown

Chapter 32   Making Tracks

China was the goal. Chinese goods were cheap and in the 1800's, they were already exporting all over the world. Early visionaries anticipated that an American transcontinental railroad would be a jugular vein of commerce between China and eastern ports.

Unfortunately, the Suez Canal was under construction using the same business model.

Nevertheless, the railroad transformed life in America.

Two companies, The Central Pacific Railroad and the Union Pacific railroad received the all-aboard signal from congress. The winning route would run from Omaha Nebraska, and Sacramento, California, to meet in an undetermined point in the middle.

The work in California began in February of 1863, but the Union Pacific was delayed until workers became available after the Civil War in 1865.

The Federal government sweetened the deal with bonds, a 400 foot corridor for the tracks and 6400 acres of adjacent land per mile of track. The railroad companies grew rich selling land long before the railroads turned a profit.

Most Californians preferred mining or farming to railroad building, so the Central Pacific hired Chinese. They proved to be well-organized and hard workers. The pay on either railroad was $30-$35 a month plus food and lodging for whites and blacks and $31 for the Chinese who did their own cooking.

Trains carried supplies to the workers at the end of the track. Mobile shanty towns called "Hell on Wheels" sprang up along the project and were famous for vice of every shade.

Safety required a maximum 2% incline grade.

As the Central Pacific chipped through the Sierras, difficult portions requiring tunnels, trestles or bridges were built by crews far ahead of the track layers. The Summit tunnel near Donner Pass was chipped and blasted through 1600 feet of solid granite high on a cliff face working from both ends and the middle, accessed by a vertical shaft. When the paths joined, they were within 2 inches of each other.

New telegraph lines were strung along the tracks for easier maintenance and repair.

Where a tunnel was too expensive, they cut a notch in a mountain. They drilled vertically to the depth required for a 2% grade, filled the holes with black powder and blasted. They hauled debris with carts to fill the next valley in the route. Where there was not enough fill from a notch, they were forced to build trestles and bridges.

The Union Pacific contracted with Brigham Young to supply Mormon crews in Utah Territory, but the Union Pacific refused to pay the workers when it was finished, claiming poverty.

Congress delayed deciding where the tracks should meet, so the competing grading teams from the east and west, both eager for land grants, passed each other and ran parallel for 200 miles.

Congress finally decided that the rails would meet at Promontory Point, Utah.

Jeff and I visited The Golden Spike Monument at Promontory Point recently. After seeing where the last spike was driven, we drove to the locomotive barn for a look at the replica engines that met there. Nearby is the site where the Central Pacific Rail Crew won a $10,000 bet for the company president by laying a record 10 miles of track in one day.

Nearby, the Big Fill trailhead sign warns to carry water and watch for rattle snakes. We hiked down to see where the two notches are cut, one by each company, not 100 feet apart. The Union built a trestle on the north side of their notch which was described in contemporary diaries as 'so rickety that it struck fear into the stoutest hearts.' The Central filled their roadbed with rock debris and the tracks were soon diverted to the safer Central path.

The China trade didn't materialize but Americans began to trade with and visit each other. "Orange trains" were kept on passenger train schedules so the fruit would be fresh when it got to points east. Industrial goods were easily carried to booming western cities. The railroad truly became the jugular vein for national prosperity.

Though trucking on interstate highways now accommodates most cargo transportation, American iron horses still move 2.2 billion tons of cargo per year. Methods have changed but prosperity still flows.

Only in America, God Bless it.

This is where the golden spike was placed.

Replicas of the two trains that met from east & west, at Promontory Point, Utah. These trains still go out on runs for special occasions.

Chapter 33   Musing From the Driver's Seat

They're in their early 20's, good looking, well-spoken college students hoping to make big money over the summer. Two of my sons and one of my daughter-in-laws have done it.

They often share an apartment with several others in their situation, including married couples. They survive on the barest comforts and diets. My son and daughter-in-law Brian and Kelsi lived in a camper on the back of a pickup truck with their two medium sized dogs. My son Chris shared a rented two bedroom house with four others. His space was a walk-in closet that just fit his camp cot.

They're Alaskan tour drivers. Cruise companies recruit teetotaler college students, supply them with a course to earn their commercial drivers licenses while they finish their spring semester. While they're learning to drive a 'coach' they begin to develop their tours. Each driver is responsible to learn all things Alaskan. Each driver develops his own tour. Chris lived in Fairbanks and sometimes drove hundreds of miles with a group, over unpaved highways and deep into the wilderness. There's a lot of time to fill and he learned to gauge when to entertain guests with stories, legends and jokes, when to inform them about geology, flora and fauna and when to give them time to rest.

 Tour guides/drivers wages are not spectacular. Wages are higher for most city bus drivers.   But Alaska is an untamed, unforgiving place, where nature reveals her spectacular beauty, but also punishes the careless.

I think my sons look better clean-shaven, but they both transformed into scruffy mountain men. I guess a beard is a powerful Alaskan talisman for earning tips.

Tourists seem to appreciate it. With the sense of needing protection in an unpredictable wilderness, the fun of a personable and well-studied (and well-washed) guide, and the thrill of seeing sights reserved for a fortunate few opens the wallets of grateful guests. Tips often outpace a driver's wages.

Tourists come from all over the world to see the gold mines, the fjords, the glaciers and wildlife. Some come to fish and to hunt while others merely gawk at the breathtaking sights, hoping for a glimpse of the great mountain, Denali, moose, elk or wolves. Of course there are some who know nothing at all about the place they have come to see, and those sorts tend to produce the most entertaining questions.

Most often the tourists are going or coming from a cruise and attach an excursion. In towns like Ketchikan or Juneau, it's a one-day adventure guaranteed to have them back on the ship before sailing. Brian and Kelsi were often asked what the elevation in Juneau was. "Well, you just got off a ship. You're standing on a dock looking at the ocean. Do you want to guess?"

 Fairbanks is inland. Visitors fly in and generally board their cruise after a few days. A Fairbanks driver was asked "So when do the deer turn into moose." It might be hard to answer that with a straight face.

They were regularly asked "Do you take American money?" (Sure! The more the merrier!) Alaska and Hawaii both became states in 1959.

Chris chuckled about having to explain many times while driving the midnight airport shuttle in the midsummer that since it was full daylight at 1:00a.m. tourists were unlikely to see the northern lights.

Hitchhikers are common. On a day off, Chris once picked up a young man who had spent the night in a remote cabin. He had no camping gear and his backpack was full of books he'd written.

Guides learn the knack of doing all they can to ensure their groups enjoy their time. They quickly learn to love the places they drive and it's fun for them when tourists enjoy it, too.

The first week of September, magical northern lights undulate in the night sky. Autumn has painted the woods for a psychedelic fiesta. Wildlife bugle and howl like a summer funeral.

The guides have returned to the rigors of school. Their bank accounts are chubby while their bodies are lean. The beards are shaved, the hair is cut. But wild Alaska is still inside.

Only in America, God bless it.

Son Chris on a day off in Alaska

View of the Prince William Sound (above), & a moose by the roadside (below).

Chapter 34   The Pig War

It all started with a pig in the garden. Any creature wrecking my vegetable garden would get the same treatment. The farmer shot him. But the difficulty arose from the fact that the garden was an American garden and the pig was an English pig. A full-out war was narrowly averted by an English admiral who had the sense to decide that his country would not go to war over a porcine murder on his orders.

Blame for the brouhaha could also be traced to an 1846 treaty that granted "everything east of "middle of the channel beside Vancouver Island" to the English and the rest, east to the Rocky Mountains following the 49th parallel, to the USA. Whether the surveyor used too thick of a quill or had too vague an understanding of the northwestern most area of "Oregon Country", we may never know, but nobody knew exactly where the border ran.

There are two channels on either side of the San Juan Islands and the unhappy pig lived in the shared area. There were American settlers, planting potatoes into which pigs could sneak, and there was the British Hudson's Bay Company running a large operation raising sheep, cattle and pigs. They'd gotten along pretty well until 1859 when that ornery pig became discontented with his usual slop.

The San Juan Islands lie on the north end of Puget Sound in Washington State. There are old growth forests and wide meadows dotted with freshwater lakes. The deep, rich soil is productive and grazing is abundant. Orcas and Minke Whales, porpoises, sea lions, seals, otters, salmon and many other fish varieties grow fat in the cold, deep water. Even today, cattle and sheep graze in postcard picturesque valleys and the woods are lovely, dark and deep.

British authorities were incensed by the handling of the errant pig. They threatened the owner of the garden, Lyman Cutlar, with arrest and then eviction for all other Americans. Americans complained to Brig. Gen. William S. Harney, who was in charge of the Oregon Territory. The general dispatched George Pickett, (later of Gettysburg fame), to defend Americans' rights to pig-free gardens.

Pickett encamped on the island with 64 soldiers. So the Brits sent Royal Navy Captain Geoffrey Hornby, three warships with a total of 62 guns, 400 Royal marines, and two handfuls of engineers with instructions to oust Pickett but to avoid war. So Pickett called for reinforcements.

Soon there were two armies facing each other, the Americans, no doubt enjoying the succulent pig. But the Royal Navy had orders not to fire on those impudent Yankees unless they were fired upon. By then, the Americans had a handsome redoubt, with 5 cannon platforms on the end of the island, (it's still there today.)

Word eventually got to Washington that the US was on the brink of a Third war with Britain over the killing of a pig. Both governments agreed to send Lt. Gen. Winfield Scott to cool the burning tempers. Once he arrived, the two sides quickly agreed to reduce each military presence to no more than 100 apiece and wait for someone to decide who truly owned the island.

They waited 12 years.

The British busied themselves building a sturdy military base, with snug, barracks, a hospital, a formal garden for herbs and flowers and a large (fenced) vegetable garden.

The Americans also built a camp, but with remarkably less style.

The imaginary war became boring, so they took breaks to celebrate Queen Victoria's birthday and the Fourth of July together.

At last, both parties asked Germany's Kaiser Wilhelm to arbitrate. The Kaiser gazed at the treaty and map through his dignified monocle and awarded the San Juan Islands to the Americans. The British gallantly took their pigs and went home.

So only one shot was fired and the casualty was a deserving pig.

Now, the San Juan Islands are romped by vacationers. Parks mark the remains of the camps. Lookout points abound for land-side whale/sea-life watching. Summer boasts an explosion of wildflowers. Kayaking tours venture out in hope of sighting resident orcas or whales. Fall colors light the woods like the sunset of summer. Recently, Jeff and I spent an afternoon there picking blackberries along rural roadsides in the tradition of marauding pigs.

Only in America, God Bless it.

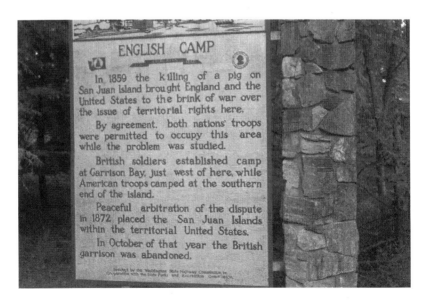

The site of the English camp on San Juan Island.

Lighthouse on San Juan Island.

Chapter 35   Land of Enchantment

By November of 2014, my nose and backside were almost perpetual popsicles. Yet, I raided the summer clothes clearance racks anticipating a two-week reprieve. We were on our way to Puerto Rico!

The island lies in the northern section of the Caribbean. Before the recent hurricanes, the mountainous island was robed in palms, flowers, dense jungle and scenic shores. The name means 'rich port' after the sheltered harbor that welcomed traders. The port itself has been guarded by an ancient fort, Castillo San Filipe del Morro, since the 16th century.

The old fort is now a world heritage site. We hiked all over the fortress from the pill box lookouts to the dungeons and barracks.

It was used actively during WW2 to defend against German submarines but became a museum in The National Park system in 1961.

Since hurricanes Irma and Maria hit Puerto Rico in quick succession, it will be awhile before they're ready for tourists again. There is no electricity up and running anywhere on the island, and entire villages have been flattened.

Though ballots have suggested that Puerto Ricans want to become a US state, they're financial problems before the storms will likely continue to prevent it. Unemployment was already over 50% for able bodied men and public assistance is more the norm than the exception. Household income is lower by half than the poorest state in the nation. Earlier this year the commonwealth of Puerto Rico entered a bankruptcy-like financial legal status, then owing over 72 billion.

So though the storms have turned everything upside down on the island territory, the resulting rebuilding could see better employment and wiser governing as the island starts over. Before the storms, they had less than half the tourism income than any of the 50 states. Many waterfront properties seemed very rundown or haphazardly built.

Yet the island is a tropical paradise! The condo we rented like an Air BnB was comfortable and clean and reasonably priced. The airport in the capital city of San Juan is modern and easy to navigate. The cobbled streets of Old San Juan are lined with quaint eateries and touristy offerings.

One evening, we took a kayak tour to a bioluminescent bay. We paddled over a smooth bay with a marina and into a mangrove forest. As the sun descended over the western edge, the channel grew dark. We switched on a red light on the back of each kayak so that we stayed in a chain behind our guide.

It was fully dark by the time we got to the bioluminescent bay. Tiny organisms live in the seawater that light up when their agitated. They're too tiny to see individually, but as the paddles pass through the water, their path alights like the Milky Way. Fish cannot hide as their gentle movement stirs the living water. Splashing Jeff's sisters and their husbands was just too fun to resist when the shower sparkled and glowed.

Another day, we hiked to a jungle waterfall in the National Forest, El Yunque. It is the only tropical rain forest in the USA. The waterfall provided a thorough drubbing on our heads, but the cold water felt delicious in the hot November morning. We swung on vines like Tarzan on our way up the trail and proceeded to a lookout tower with terrific jungle and coastal views.

Along the highways there are stretches of open air food stands, most selling mofongo, the quintessential Puerto Rican food. It's mashed plantains mixed with onions and meat and other savory flavorings and then deep fried. There were more deep fried traditional offerings than a county fair. The food generally is similar to Cajun with lots of tomatoes, onions, peppers and beans. Traditional meats are pork and chicken and seafood.

Puerto Rico is a US territory, so its natives are US citizens. The difference is that they pay no federal income taxes and do not vote in national elections. Citizens can travel freely between Puerto Rico and any part of the USA without a passport.

The Puerto Rican landscape has been decimated. But nature will find a way and the island will heal. Its nickname, "The Enchanted Island" will apply again and she will once again be clothed in flowering jungles. Hopefully the Rich Port will be better than ever,

Only in America, God Bless it.

Kayaking at the bioluminescent bay

Getting ready to swim under the waterfall at El Yunque.

El Morro in Old San Juan

Chapter 36   Going Exploring

They seem like an ordinary family. Three sons and a daughter, a beautiful home that they have enjoyed finishing. Sports leagues, a church congregation, Dad works and Mom stays home with the kids.

But that started to change for Brandon and Nichole Bruce about 6 years ago. It started with food. What virtue was there in the typical American diet? They spent too much and ate too much of the wrong things.

So they changed. They cut back on meats, treats and ready-made foods and emphasized a more plant-based diet. They feel healthier and spend less.

Spending less on food also pointed out that though Brandon earns an ample income, they had unnecessary debt. Again, they asked themselves why. So they destroyed the credit cards and started paying off their loans, from smallest to largest until they have no debt except their mortgage.

Aw, the mortgage. Even with the lifestyle changes already in place, they both had the sense that they were missing out. They read about a family on social media that sold an app for millions, uprooted their kids and became world travelers. An idea began to germinate.

The only problem was that they didn't have millions of dollars. And they did have a mortgage. But Brandon is a web designer and realized that there was no important reason for him to work in an office. But he couldn't seem to land a new job that would accommodate world travel.

Brandon had been raised in a military family and had seen a bit of the world. But neither he nor Nichole had seen much of the eastern or any of the southern part of the USA. As soon as they turned their attention to a new US based plan, things began falling into place.

Brandon was hired by a company that was fine with him designing websites from wherever he chose. The children began helping research potential stops on their year of adventure. Brandon has always been interested in American history, but Nichole began to discover the wonders and diversity the USA offers for the first time.

Nichole's and Bruce's parents had varied levels of enthusiasm to their plan. Friends also responded differently. Brandon explained that many would say, "Why?" He answered simply "Why not?" Others say, "I could never do that!" and again they wonder, "Why not?"

They started simplifying their home décor and furnishings, aiming for a minimalist effect. As they embarked last Friday, they had sold or donated over half the house contents. They are driving only a minivan and will store their remaining belongings in one spare bedroom and a basement storage room in their home.

They easily found ideal renters that will occupy the house for the year they are absent. The rent will cover the cost of their lodgings elsewhere.

The last hurdle was the children's education. Nichole struggled to find an ideal homeschool curriculum. One day as she walked for exercise, she met an acquaintance, Mary, that she knew homeschooled. As she asked her questions and Mary showed her how it all worked in their family, Nichole realized she'd found the perfect fit.

Braxton is the oldest and has just started Jr. High. He was hesitant to leave his routine life and the security of his friends. But once his parents asked him to help choose destinations, he got excited. He is eager to see Hershey, Pennsylvania, and his 18 month younger brother Isaac is most excited for the month they will be in New York City. Six-year-old Zoey is most eager to live in lots of different houses and 3 year old Beckett has packed his backpack for an 'inventure.'

Brandon is eager to try new traditional foods in the various locales and Nichole is most eager for new adventures and experiences.

The children have attended public schools up until last Thursday when they said their goodbyes. Friday, they started for their first destination, New Braunfels, Texas, in the hill country near San Antonio.

They will spend the winter in the warmer climes of the south, enjoying new beaches, history, flora and fauna. They will attend church in each locale and include the children in the weekday activities. Their object is to experience as many cultures, and places as they can pack into a year.

Americana will share their adventures with regular updates, features and photos.

They're doing it because they can.

Only in America, God bless it.

The Bruce Family, just prior to the start of their adventure

Beth M Stephenson

Chapter 37   Clever, Cute or Funny

With Halloween upon us, my mind turns to pranks. Not the low-down dirty rotten nasty kind, but the clever, well-thought out variety that makes the target laugh, once they get it. I'm not talking psycho nut cases scarring their victims for life, just a momentary startle or bit of confusion until we realize we've been had.

As with all national cultures around the globe, we have our own brand of funny.

There's the inadvertent prank like the one my brother Mark played on my husband the other day. Mark came back from a day of fishing with his grandkids while he and his wife, Catherine were staying with us. He put his carton of worms into our fridge with my permission. But to Jeff, it looked like an ordinary yogurt carton. He went to help himself to some yogurt and opened a very unexpected can of worms.

My friend Sue Monson has a plastic skeleton that she poses around the house to surprise her husband. Sometimes Bones is on the pot with a book, in his closet styling a purse or waving cheerfully from the driver's seat of his truck.

My sons also show pranking prowess by adding a dose of subtlety to magnify dramatic impact.

Once they stowed our youngest, Thomas, in the clothes dryer. Then Scott seemed to shower and then called for me to bring him a towel. I was busy writing, so I passed the request to one of the younger boys upstairs. My boys were pretty obedient, but this time, the child I asked refused.

"Please, Mom!" Scott begged. "I'm cold!" I marched upstairs, chastising the whole lot of them. In the laundry room, another son was flopped over the clean clothes, which made me even madder. I reached into the drier, mid-scolding and Thomas grabbed my hand.

Oh the cheers and laughter that followed my scream! The boy who had requested the towel had secretly followed me up (fully dressed) to enjoy the full impact. That success set off a rash of harmless pranks around our house.

Another time, the two oldest boys set up a ladder outside the bathroom where our daughter Tricia would soon be starting her nightly face cleaning routine. All they did was look in the window and wait for her to notice their reflection in the mirror. When she did notice, her scream conjured visions of a murder scene.

Then there was the time my natal family was camping and my little brother Jim stood on a bluff above me while I sunbathed. It was chilly, yet I was suddenly showered with warm water. Across the lake, the fishermen heard a furious scream, an evil laugh, a resounding spank and a wail. That incident does NOT qualify as either harmless or funny.

Every year, it seems someone in the neighborhood will get 'toilet papered'. The prank is to wait until the darkest night and unfurl miles of toilet paper over the victims' house, and property.

The best prank in our family lore was a time the tables turned on the Toilet Paperers. On the night before Thanksgiving, our sons Daniel and Chris suspected a toilet papering event was planned for our house. The Toilet Paperers were known to be extremely thorough.

Just after midnight our boys watched two figures clad in black sneak into our front yard. They hauled two huge trash bags filled with toilet paper. Our boys eased the window open and slunk into the cover of the shrubs. Just as the visitors opened their sacks and flung the first rolls, our kids let fly with their paintball guns. Both visitors were full-grown but one was 6'7"and 300 lbs, so they were easy targets.

There were a few moments of confusion, followed by terror. Paintballs sting and the Paperers thought someone was shooting real ammo. The Bigger Intruder fled around the corner of the house where Daniel grabbed him from behind, pinning his arms, but not speaking. He wriggled free and they fled up the street, leaving about 80 rolls of toilet paper behind.

A few days later, revenge was complete when our boys (unbeknownst to me) used the captured toilet paper to smother the master Toilet Paperer's house.

Pranking American style: harmless, funny, and clever.

Only in America, God bless it.

Beth M Stephenson

Chapter 38   The Space Needle

I grew up watching reruns of Hanna-Barbera's *The Jetsons*, and eventually became aware that their flying saucer home was patterned after a real-life structure. I hoped I would someday visit it.

New York has the Empire State Building, Paris has the Eiffel Tower. San Francisco has the Golden Gate Bridge but perhaps the most easily identifiable structure in the USA is Seattle's Space Needle. Built in 1962 for the World's Fair, it was the tallest structure west of the Mississippi at the time.

Recently, armed with our Seattle CityPasses, Jeff and I eagerly boarded the Monorail downtown. The Space Needle is the only stop, so it's impossible to get lost.

I love unique architecture and I felt a little giddy at the foot of such an iconic, soaring structure. Everywhere around the giant base, people were aiming their cameras heavenward. We exchanged our CityPass coupons at a kiosk for timed tickets and joined the line for the ride up. We entertained ourselves with the photographic displays while we waited 15 minutes to board the high-speed elevators.

The Space Needle was built to be a symbol as well as a tourist attraction. Guides give a necessarily short overview on the 520 foot ride up to the observation deck and then let you explore the views and displays on your own.

The original idea by businessman Edward E Carlson was conceived as he dined in a rotating restaurant in Germany. The Seattle World's Fair needed just such an attraction, he thought.

His first concept resembled a lollypop or tethered balloon more than the graceful Needle.

The design was quickly altered when architect John Graham, tasked with the actual production of the Needle, got involved. He changed the bulb-on-a-stick idea to a flying saucer. The Needle would have a restaurant with a 14 foot ring near the windows so perfectly balanced that its rotation takes less than an hour and is powered by a tiny 1 ½ horsepower motor.

The pedestal was the next design question. A single tower lacked grace as well as necessary stability so Victor Steinbrueck created the hourglass-shaped tripod pedestal.

Nearby, a futuristic monorail was under construction connecting downtown Seattle with a station directly adjacent to the Needle site. The project was nearly scrapped when builders failed to find a suitable site inside the fair grounds. But at the last minute, they noticed a defunct fire and police dispatch station site, just 120 feet square that financiers bought for $75K.

By the time the land was purchased, the opening of the fair was just about 15 months away. The 120 foot foundation was poured all in a day, sunk 30 feet in the ground. The structure that soon began to rise from the concrete anchor was bolted down with 72 bolts, each 30 feet long. The foundation contains 250 tons of steel reinforcements and 5600 tons of concrete.

The Needle itself weighs just 3700 tons. The halo's diameter is broader than its foundation by 18 feet but the entire structure's center of gravity is just 5 feet above ground level. The Space Needle is built to withstand a category 5 hurricane or over a 9.1 earthquake without significant damage.

The Needle was finished just 2 days before the 1962 World's Fair opened. Almost 20,000 people per day of the fair visited the Observation Deck.

During the Fair, the Needle also boasted a gigantic torch. It burned natural gas and was a "futuristic" prediction that natural gas would become a normal part of life. But the flame became unpopular for its wastefulness and was replaced by a powerful beam that is still lit on special occasions each year.

The Seattle skyline has changed in the last 55 years. Now, skyscrapers are common and many of the futuristic dreams embodied by the Needle are indeed part of everyday life. As Jeff and I explored the colossal structure I felt the optimism and imagination that had produced it and so many other American achievements. It seemed like physical proof that if someone can imagine it, someone can also create it.

Bruce Family Update: Zoey was very excited to visit the Four Corners, the only place in the USA where four states meet. She wanted to stand in New Mexico, Colorado, Arizona and Utah all at once. She got her wish at the very beginning of the Bruce's year of adventure!

Only in America, God bless it.

View of the Space Needle from the water

Monorail to the Space Needle

Chapter 39 A Silver Lining to a Terrible War

The War Between the States claimed more American lives than all other American wars put together. It devastated the country and the effects still influence modern culture and policy.

But as with most tragedies, there were a few beneficial side effects. The most far-reaching and important benefit was the gruesome fact that with all of the devastating injuries, medical science and anatomical knowledge leapt forward. Until then, physicians had sometimes resorted to grave robbing for the sake of studying human anatomy.

But a more subtle advance was the building of new kinds of ships. One of those was a craft built by the Confederate States of America which carried 8 men. One was the pilot and the others cranked the shaft that propelled the vessel. She was named *The H. L. Hunley* after her designer and builder, Horace Hunley.

The *Hunley* was not the first functioning submarine. In the Revolutionary war, George Washington's army had a little one man craft called the *Turtle*, built by American inventor, David Bushnell.

 Its function was slightly different, as the ordinance was to be attached directly to the hull and then detonated via a timer. It nearly succeeded, but in the midnight waters of the Hudson River, the pilot couldn't see. He tried to attach the bomb to the wrong place on the ship's hull and when that didn't work, he aborted the mission. Two more tries failed for other reasons. The craft itself functioned perfectly and the concept was only forfeited when the boat carrying *The Turtle* was sunk.

The Hunley holds the distinction of being the first submarine to succeed in its military mission. She sank the Union USS Housatonic near the mouth of Charleston S.C. harbor. Once certain of their success, the crew signaled shore of their success and then disappeared. Searches yielded nothing. Craft and crew had vanished.

Clive Cussler, a popular American author, funds marine archeology by selling his adventure books. His National Underwater and Marine Agency hunts for shipwrecks of historical significance. Cussler wanted the Hunley in the worst way and returned multiple times to the area where he strongly suspected she was entombed.

They found *The H.L. Hunley* in 1995. After 136 years underwater, she was encased in concretion formed of barnacles and sand.

The painstaking *Hunley* project proceeds at the Warren Lasch Conservation Center in North Charleston, SC. The WLCC is part of Clemson University and the facility focuses on advancing and finding best practices in preserving and studying materials of historical significance. She has slowly emerged from her encasement.

I feel for them. Once as a young teen, my Dad offered me $10 to chip the barnacles off the bottom of our homemade ocean fishing boat. The *Hunky Dory* was a mere 29 feet long and only the area below the waterline needed to be cleaned. It was gruesome work, like chipping concrete that stunk like dead fish. The trick was to use enough force to get the superglued barnacles off without damaging the hull underneath. I can only imagine what it would be like if the surface underneath was a priceless and irreplaceable artifact.

The Hunley was built of cast and wrought iron. The hull has deteriorated to a fragile shell, liable to break away under the slightest over-exertion. The craft is preserved in a 75000 gallon tank of chemical solution to prevent her rusting into oblivion. Before they work, they drain the tank, wrap the craft in plastic wrap and then work as fast as they can to minimize the time exposed to air.

Archeologists do have accurate drawings of the ship. They knew which materials were used where and which parts were likely to be forensic hot spots.

In 2015, after removing 1200 pounds of concretion, the exterior hull was completely exposed. Researchers found evidence that the torpedo explosion that sank the USS Housatonic may also have fatally damaged the submarine.

Though the interior of the craft is similarly encrusted, the bodies of the crew were already buried in 2004.

Scientists have already uncovered the surprisingly sophisticated engineering of the crank mechanism. Other clues raise additional questions and possibilities. But the yen to find the truth of our American history draws them forward in the painstaking project to uncover the secrets of The *Hunley.*

Only in America, God bless it.

Jeff and Chris with replica of the Hunley in Charleston, South Carolina.

Beth M Stephenson

Chapter 40   The Magical Underground

We lumbered along over the rolling, green hills of Texas in our ancient motorhome. It was July 4th and we intended to celebrate by watching a cloud of bats launch into the dusky sky from the mouth of Carlsbad Caverns. But the serpentine belt broke and we were delayed several hours as we waited for an angel mechanic to bring and install the part we needed and charge us very little. That old motorhome had a knack for bringing out the very best of Good Samericans.

But we missed the bats. It was long after dark by the time we rolled into a gravel parking spot for the night. I was too tired to get up at 4:00 a.m. to see the bats return. The cave, a national park since 1930, would have to be enough.

It was hard to believe that the almost featureless desert landscape covered a vast magical wonderland underground. Though Carlsbad Caverns includes 119 caves, only three have tours and only the biggest has elevators, lights, and even a café.

They form through chemical reactions forming acid that eats away the limestone from a prehistoric reef on an inland sea. The tectonic plates thrust the land upward and the water drained out of the caverns. Then freshwater leached through the upper soil and rock dissolves the lime. When it touches the air of the cavern, it solidifies into formations.

Stalactites hang from the ceiling (they hold 'tite') and stalagmites rise from the floor. But air currents and water currents combined with seismic movement work together to form other fantastical and netherworldly formations.

Other formations are called soda straws and corkscrews. In some caves, the formations grow sideways and twist as the wind currents have their way with them. Others flow into striped forms that resemble giant slabs of bacon.

Regardless of the science, it's an enchanted place with ornate fairytale palaces, hidden pools so still and clear that it's hard to perceive the water. I felt like an ant touring a pirate treasure chest with giant sparkling gems and crystals everywhere.

We did see a few stray bats near the natural entrance and they added a touch of dark magic, too. They're wonderful for controlling insects, but Halloween has forever tainted their reputation. But how can I cringe at a creature that lives in nature's cathedral.

It seems strange too that all of the spectacular beauty develops in utter darkness, waiting like a Christmas present for someone to discover and enjoy it.

I can only imagine what Jim White thought when he first explored it. He went to investigate when he saw what he thought was a black dust devil spiraling up at the same time each day. He climbed down into the blackness on a homemade wire ladder.

The cave has kept many of the names Jim White gave the rooms, including The Big Room. It is indeed the largest in the Cave system, measuring 4,000 feet long and 625 feet wide. He got a little more creative when he named the New Mexico Room, Kings Palace, Queens Chamber, and Papoose Room. He had some fun with some of the more distinct formations, naming them the Totem Pole, Witch's Finger, Giant Dome, Bottomless Pit, Fairyland, Iceberg Rock, Rock of Ages and Temple of the Sun. White continued to be part of Carlsbad Caverns development though out his life.

The bats forsake the cave just before Halloween and return in mid-April. When present, most of them live in the no-frills, undecorated pad called the Bat Cave.

The bat guano at Carlsbad Caverns was one of the first commercial attractions. The bat poop is so high in nitrogen that it's highly prized as fertilizer. Early spelunkers (the sport of cave exploring) lowered themselves in guano baskets.

Another cave in the complex is the Lechugilla Cave. Uncommercial and utterly pristine, it is accessible through scientific permit only and contains over 100 miles of mapped passages including the deepest area of the cave system at 1600 feet. There are other caves in the system accessible to genuine spelunkers looking for adventure.

Carlsbad Caverns is neither the biggest nor the deepest cave system in the US, but it's a gloriously beautiful national treasure, glittering just below the desert of New Mexico.

Only in America, God bless it.

Sons Brian, Daniel and Thomas at the entrance to Carlsbad Caverns.

Chapter 41   Thanksgivings

The Bruce family has been exploring Texas and getting adjusted to their new travelling lifestyle. They've particularly enjoyed swimming and river floating activities. Nichole reports that the homeschooling took a bit of tweaking at first. The hardest part is that the youngest, Beckett, is too young to sit and color during school hours. Also, lessons that are appropriate for the older are too advanced for Zoey. But Nichole is enjoying teaching the children and watching them learn and improve each day. The kids like the fact that school is only about 4 hours.

The best part of all is that the kids play together and fighting is almost non-existent. They've visited state parks, The Alamo, and enjoyed the local history of New Braunfels. They will move to Gulf Shores, Alabama this week for a new chapter. They don't have specific Thanksgiving plans yet.

As I prepared the Thanksgiving menu this year, the ghosts of Thanksgivings Past rose up from their graves and grinned at me.

One of the ugliest was the second Thanksgiving in the first home we owned. It was a little place that needed a lot of work before it was comfortably livable. By our second Thanksgiving there, our number 4 child was 15 months old, but I wanted to host my in-laws.

The problem was that I had one small oven and nobody lived close enough to bring hot food.

My foodie friend, Richard Pike, praised the method of barbequing the bird. He described the moist, succulent meat, falling off the bone in smoky slabs of deliciousness. "The only thing you have to do is make your gravy separately. The meat tastes fantastic with the smoky flavor, but it ruins the gravy," he said.

He gave me careful instructions in placing the coals in the new barbeque my in-laws had given us for Christmas the year before. I followed instructions precisely, basting, turning, and replenishing the coals.

In the meantime, I followed a tight schedule for all the side dishes taking turns in the oven, with the rolls last of all. Nothing is better than rolls steaming in a basket just as the blessing is asked.

The meal preparation ticked along like a well-greased machine. Green bean casserole, sweet potatoes and apples, dressing, and as the Turkey was ready to begin its post-roasting rest, I popped in the tall soft potato rolls.

The tables were set for 12. Jeff sliced into the turkey. Horrors! The meat was still quite pink! I rushed it back to the coals hoping that 30 minutes would transform the raw-looking meat.

But it was the same after half an hour and the half hour after that. I revved up the coals hot enough to roast Shadrack, Meshak and Abednego, but after an extra hour and a half, the meat was still pink.

The side dishes were cold. My mother-in-law suggested we go ahead without the turkey and so we reheated a few things a bit. By then, it had been 2 hours since the promised dinner-time.

I decided to carve the turkey and finish off the process with a bit of nuking in our new-to-us microwave.

When the turkey came from the microwave, dry as a desert and still pink, I realized that barbequing poultry leaves the meat pink, even when it's thoroughly cooked. And that turkey had been quite cooked for 2 hours.

It was a much bigger failure to me than to our guests. We all laughed about it and several confessed that the turkey is their least favorite part of the meal anyway. That year, it was everybody's least favorite, no doubt.

Another year, I went a little crazy baking pies. The day before Thanksgiving, I let everybody choose their favorite and ended up with 11 pies. There were only 9 in the family, but the pumpkin recipe makes two and the razzleberry makes 3. So my oven was on for the entire Wednesday before the holiday.

I rose early on Thanksgiving to stuff and inter the Traditional Tom in the roasting pan. But by 10:00 o'clock, I should have been smelling the turkey and I wasn't.

There's nothing so hideous as raw turkey just 2 hours from mealtime. Turns out that the oven igniter had gone bad (on Thanksgiving of all times!). Happily, the broiler still worked and by clever manipulating, we tricked the oven into eventually doing its job.

We Americans have so many wonderful things to be thankful for. A blip or two in a feast or a disappointing day are nothing compared with the opportunities, comforts, and peace we enjoy.

Only in America, God Bless it!

Beth M Stephenson

Chapter 42   Remember the Alamo

Long before the fifes would play and the drums would beat for the American Revolution, Spanish Catholics built missions in the remote niches of New Spain. One such was near the river they named 'San Antonio.' They began with living quarters for the priests and soon added outbuildings for the cattle.

They taught the native people Catholicism and converts began gathering near the developing compound. Eventually, walls were constructed to protect the converts from raiding Apaches and Comanche's. A church, built of 4 foot thick limestone blocks, was begun.

The chapel was planned to be a typical cruciform, with the long nave and short transepts forming a Christian cross. It was to have twin bell towers, a domed roof and niches for statuary.

 As America fought England in the east, unrest spread in the west and south. Spanish Commandant Teodoro de Croix declared that all unbranded cattle belonged to the government. Apaches had stolen most of the mission horses so there was no way for the pueblo to round up cattle for branding. The mission complex and the unfinished chapel were abandoned.

But where it had failed as a mission, it was reborn as a military outpost. During the 1821 war between Spain and Mexico which resulted in Mexico's independence, the old mission was used as a hospital and later as a prison. American settlers moved into the area and renamed the fort for the cottonwood trees that grew nearby. The Spanish word for Cottonwood is 'Alamo.'

Mexican soldiers garrisoned there until Texian settlers, wearied of Mexico's heavyhandedness, started a rebellion for independence.

Sam Houston ordered Col. James Bowie to demolish the Alamo because it was poorly designed for use as a fort. But there were too many cannons for the available oxen to move, and Bowie convinced Gov. Sam Houston that the fort's location had strategic value.

By February of 1836, an army of about 200 Texian soldiers occupied the old mission-turned-fort. Col. James Bowie and Lt. Col William Travis shared command.

A bloodthirsty man named Santa Anna had alternately ruled all of Mexico and commanded Mexico's military. He commanded 1800 Mexican soldiers, mostly forcibly constricted, to surround The Alamo. David Crockett was among those trapped in the fort. (He never went by 'Davy' until he got to Hollywood.)

Mexico had declared that all rebel Texians were pirates, were to be given no quarter and executed if captured. Messengers from inside The Alamo snuck out to beg Texas leaders for reinforcements.

Reinforcements were promised. So rather than abandon an indefensible fort, the volunteer soldiers waited and hoped. But help never came.

Early in the morning of March 6, 1836, William Travis drew a line in the sand with his saber, inviting any who would fight and die with him in the cause of freedom to cross it. Most did.

Santa Anna commanded an attack. The first and second waves were repulsed, but each time a Texian rose above the wall to fire, he was outlined against the sky like a target for practice.

Before midday the Texians were dead. Eyewitnesses described Santa Anna's soldiers shooting and bayoneting dead bodies long after the battle ceased. A few Texians tried to surrender but Santa Anna commanded their immediate execution.

David Crockett is dead. James Bowie was too sick to rise from his bed and is found dead in his quarters. William Travis is dead. 600 of Santa Anna's men are dead, nearly tripling the number of dead Americans.

Santa Anna burned the bodies of the vanquished. The common Christian belief was that only a whole body could be resurrected. News of the massacre and brutality spread and Texas volunteers flocked to join Sam Houston's army. Just six weeks later American Texians shouted "Remember the Alamo" as they charge into San Jacinto, the final battle for freedom from Mexico.

Santa Anna is defeated. The Republic of Texas is born. In 1845 Texas was annexed into the USA as the 28th state.

The now-famous bell-shaped front façade of the chapel and a domed roof was added by the US Army just before the Civil War.

Now the free, Word Heritage Site is swarmed with millions of visitors each year. My family was there in the brutal heat of a summer day and The Alamo was one of the first sites visited by the adventuring Bruce family.

Only in America, God Bless it.

Beth M Stephenson

Chapter 43   The American Red Cross

If the road to Hell is paved with good intentions, I joined the wrong road crew.

I love to kick off the holiday season with some sort of service activity. I saw an ad on TV commenting on those who have survived the disasters all over the world this year. The advertisement explained that there are still many people without power in Puerto Rico. It struck me that rather than doing something grandiose, I could always donate blood. Holiday parties often lead to more car accidents which lead to a need for more blood.

It was easy to find a donation site. I googled the Red Cross and found half a dozen upcoming blood drives. There was one nearby this very day, so Jeff and I made appointments.

Unfortunately we'd never been on the college campus where the blood drive was going on. It took us 20 minutes to find a legal place to park. Then we had to walk to the far side of the campus, asking directions along the way before we finally saw the lovely red cross on a white background with a helpful little arrow to guide us.

I admit it's been a long time since I gave blood. I think I was turned down the last time because of anemia. But once we had read several pages of information, we waited to be officially screened.

The worker took my blood pressure, (104 over 68) asked my weight, (000) took my pulse (70) and then pricked my left ring finger, drawing out a tiny bit of blood he put in a machine. I passed!

I was feeling quite proud of myself when he turned the computer over to me so I could answer some questions. I was sailing through with a clear conscience until I got to the question about travelling out of the country.

Now, lest you think I'm a dimwit for not thinking of it sooner, I had called the Red Cross help line and had already determined that our trip to Equador a couple weeks ago didn't pose a problem. Apparently, none of the areas we visited had elevated malaria risks.

But then the cute little phlebotomist asked "Anywhere else?"

I had almost forgotten our trip to Thailand and China. But I fessed up. Who knew that malaria can live hidden in your bloodstream for up to a year without causing symptoms? I could hear that Jeff was encountering the same problem in the next booth.

The rules are strict and absolute. I know I didn't get any bug bites on that trip, but that didn't matter. We had to find our itinerary buried on our phones to recall the names of the places we'd gone.

It was our trip to the Bridge over the River Kwai that eliminated us. That region of Thailand is apparently prone to malaria. "We still want you to have some cookies," the friendly Red Cross worker, Katherine, told us.

But I had too much pride to raid the treat table after being rejected as a blood donor. We hiked back to our car, hoping that it is indeed the 'thought that counts.'

Now every time I have a hot flash, I'll think I've caught malaria, but I learned some interesting facts.

The Red Cross originated at the first Geneva Convention of 1864. It set forth the mission of the autonomous humanitarian organization named Red Cross and its articles were signed as an international treaty. It focused first on relieving injured soldiers and protecting prisoners but eventually morphed into a worldwide organization with chapters in 195 countries. In non-Christian countries, it is called The Red Crescent. In Israel, it's the Red Star of David.

Shortly after the first Geneva Convention, Clara Barton started the American charter of the Red Cross. Today, ARC has half a million volunteers and about 30,000 employees. They train about 12 million people in first aid each year and are the largest supplier of blood and blood products in the US. They are organized to give relief to disaster and crisis survivors. Blood donations not only supply a safe blood supply, but provide funding to the Red Cross for other humanitarian efforts.

The ARC totals about 67,000 disaster responses annually, with the most common being house fires. They have an excellent ratio of money spent on relief vs overhead.

They wouldn't take our blood, but I'll bet they'll accept our money. That might be an even easier way to buy some holiday cheer.

Only in America, God bless it.

Beth M Stephenson

Chapter 44   A 4-H Leader that Changed Christmas

 I heard on the news that the 2017 Black Friday sales broke records for dollars spent at about 5 Billion dollars. Some forecasters said that they expected cyber Monday and the following week to also break records at around 6 Billion.

That's a lot of money. The trend of Christmas shopping is to online sources, but brick and mortar stores are still doing fine. Yet behind the scenes, Pinterest is exploding with tutorials for those that opt for a homemade Christmas.

Growing up in a large family without much extra money, I often made the majority of my gifts and so did Santa. Many years, we children were barred from the garage where Dad had his workshop for weeks before the magical night.

My childhood Christmas giving budget was usually only a few dollars. Then, it was much cheaper to buy materials and make something spectacular than it was to buy the finished product. That age is returning with access online to cool things for crafting.

I think it was that mindset of making things I wanted and couldn't afford to buy that made me eager to join 4-H. We got a flyer in our 3rd grade class. I could hardly believe my eyes! I could take sewing and cooking!

4-H had been around since 1902. It had originally started as a method of helping farmers accept new agricultural developments from University research. Apparently the older farmers resisted change to their methods, and youth were eager to try new things.

By the late 60's when I first joined, they had branched out as not only an agricultural organization, but to promoting all homemaking skills. It was focused largely in rural areas. Now, 4-H is a youth organization that focuses on developing life skills including engineering, computer and other sciences, agriculture and homemaking skills.

The volunteer teachers were both parents of my classmates. I was nervous about that. It was one thing to chase boys on the playground and another to actually go into Kelly Hartsell's house. The issue almost made me change my mind.

But Kelly didn't seem too overwrought by my getting off the bus with him. He grabbed a quick snack and then vanished for the duration.

Mrs. Hartsell told us she had decided to become a 4-H volunteer because she loved to sew and had no daughters to teach.

She was a born teacher with endless patience and complete competence. We started with clever   drawstring bags. They were ideal for practicing sewing straight seams. Mrs Hartsell only accepted our best effort. Afterall, the motto of 4-H is 'Head, Hands, Heart and Health.' That seemed to imply that we gave only our best effort. She insisted that we redo our mistakes until they were properly accomplished. If one girl became frustrated, Mrs. Hartsell's stalwart patience triumphed in the end.

 By the time I was done with her class, I knew how to use a pattern and had made a drawstring bag, a skirt, a jumper and a pant suit. A fashionista was born!

 By Christmastime, I was proficient enough to sew on my own at home. I anticipated the delight in my family as they each opened a lovely drawstring bag. At last Dad would have somewhere to put his nails and screws, my brothers could use them for marbles or baseball cards.

I remember that I folded each bag differently so nobody would guess that everyone was getting the same thing.

Finally the Day of Wonder arrived. My mother instantly saw the possibility for storing her lipsticks. Dad also claimed to have immediate need for just such a bag. Filled with the Spirit of Christmas Diplomacy, my siblings followed suit.

It was a happy day. Santa brought me a sewing kit with my very own scissors, pincushion, pins, measuring tape and tailor's ruler. Oh ecstasies!

The next year, I had learned to make candles at school. I spent my Christmas money on a squirrel candle mold, paraffin, crayons and cotton string.

This year, as I sew dresses for my granddaughters and craft bead creations for some of the women of my family, I'm grateful again to Mrs. Hartsell who gave me her time, knowledge and patience. I also just learned that there are active 4-H chapters near my home. Hmmmmm.

Only in America, God Bless it.

Beth M Stephenson

Chapter 45   An American White Christmas

A "perfect hurricane" described the terrible weather that Christmas night. Rain needled into ice and turned to sleet and snow. Thousands of men huddled a little west of the Delaware River in Pennsylvania. They were a discouraged mix of the Continental Army and state militias.

The cause of liberty was not going well. The British had whipped Washington's army in New York. Traitors like Benedict Arnold cut them off at the knees. Desertion was rampant and many contracts ended with the year. It was Christmas and the men were hungry, cold and low on munitions.

Yet Thomas Paine had just published his pamphlet that began, "These are the times that try men's souls," depicting deserters and quitters as unpatriotic, faithless cowards. George Washington ordered the pamphlet read aloud to every soldier. It had succeeded in raising morale a bit, but reinforcements brought food and warm blankets. Congress seemed to catch a bit of Christmas spirit and resupplied the army.

General Washington surmised that if America was ever to triumph in the cause of freedom, they must begin immediately with some victories.

The object of the secret plan was a garrison of about 1400 Hessians. Hessians had been crucial in calamitous defeats earlier in the year. They were known to be well-trained fighting men. Famed for looting and pillaging, their cruelty had inspired many local men to join Washington's army in recent weeks.

The Hessians at Trenton, New Jersey were part of the 17 thousand soldiers rented by the British to help fight the

American war. Germanic princes had been lining their pockets by renting out their armies for hundreds of years. The American war was particularly lucrative so sovereigns had rounded up not only criminals, the dimwitted and troublemakers, but also farmers and tradesmen.

Yet when the spy's message reached Hessian commander Dall, informing him that Washington was planning to cross the Delaware and attack, he ignored it. It was Christmas! And besides that, a powerful nor'easter gathered strength. The Delaware River lay between the armies and it was treacherous with ice.

Washington's plan was to have three divisions cross the Delaware at different points. In the south, they would create a diversion and in the north, they were to cut off Hessian retreat.

The password that Christmas night was 'Victory or Death.'

Washington himself would lead 2500 men across the river and march them 10 miles south to Trenton. They were to go as quietly as possible. Washington had procured every water craft in the region and planned to use ferries to haul heavy artillery and horses. The men would float in high-sided, shallow-drafted Durham boats used for hauling ore. Skilled boat handlers from Maine and other areas were among their ranks, ready to maneuver the crafts safely. Not one boat was lost.

With a ten-mile march in a howling snowstorm awaiting them on the far side of the river, it was crucial to keep dry. Water sloshed in the bottoms of the Durham boats, so the men stood. Huge chunks of ice crashed into the boats, knocking a few soldiers into the water.

It was 4 a.m by the time the patriots and their artillery had crossed the Delaware. Washington's careful plan was 3 hours behind schedule. The General was tempted to retreat. Had he known that his enemy had been informed and that the supporting divisions deployed north and south had been turned back by the storm, he would likely have given up.

But the same raging storm that nearly stymied Washington lulled the Hessians into enjoying their Christmas rum. The Americans arrived in Trenton around 8:00 a.m. and found even the Hessian guards still nestled all snug in their beds.

The battle was a quick, decisive victory. 22 Hessians were killed and almost 900 taken prisoner. Commander Dall was mortally wounded.

Emboldened by their resounding victory, Washington's army pushed forward throughout the week, achieving more important victories and turning the tide of the war toward liberty.

If the Christmas of 1776 had not been a white Christmas, Americans would likely be singing God Save the Queen at Cricket matches and driving on the wrong side of the road.

Only in America, God bless it.

Beth M Stephenson

Chapter 46   The Adventuring Bruce Family Enjoys a Stress-free Season

The Brandon and Nichole Bruce family have just left Gulf Shore AL and are now in Santa Rosa Beach FL.

Nichole writes: "At a time of year that is usually filled with Christmas parties, church activities, school activities, and tons of running around, we find ourselves noticeably un-busy, calm and joyful. We've found fun ways to serve those around us. We are watching all the Star Wars movies in anticipation for the new movie coming out. We've gone on train rides to see Santa and watched a holiday boat parade. It's been pretty incredible to just slow down and enjoy this season."

While most Americans told Gallup pollsters that they intended to spend more this Christmas than last, the most on average in a decade, the Bruce family is in the mode to spend both time and money meaningfully. This year they are avoiding the traditions and demands that often make the holiday season stressful, especially for parents.

They have continued the traditions started a few years ago of giving experiences or games that they can enjoy as a family instead of showering their children with more stuff. In fact they have found that even though they brought only the belongings that fit in a minivan, they feel they brought along more stuff than they need. "Every time we pack up, we look at what we've got and see if there's anything that isn't being used. If there is, that item gets donated or thrown away."

But she does have some regrets. "I wish we would have brought my kids razor scooters, but other than that I wish we would have brought less. We will probably be sending some things home."

As a new homeschooler, Nichole says they're in the groove now. "We took a field trip this week to see a WWII battleship and submarine in Mobile AL. My Grandpa is a submarine veteran and I loved seeing the inside of a submarine. We just finished up our Space unit and we are excited to go the Pensacola naval aviation museum this weekend. We are adding in more fun electives like Art, learning Spanish and coding. The part of homeschooling that I'm enjoying is learning right along with my kids: History, grammar, reading, etc. I also enjoy the conversations we are having outside of school time. I know what they're learning so we can talk about it anytime something comes up throughout our day."

The Bruces chartered a boat one Saturday while they were in Gulf Shores. Nichole writes, "They took us out to the ocean and we saw a couple baby dolphins and their moms. They also showed us how they fish for shrimp (it's not shrimp season), and we caught some different kinds of fish. We even caught a sting ray, which our captain tagged and threw back into the ocean. We came in just as the sun was setting and the Super moon was rising." Nichole said that activity was probably the family favorite from Gulf Shores.

They're enjoying a Christmas season with temperatures in the 60's, and they loved the slow pace of the Gulf Shores lifestyle. Traffic and businesses were quieter and slower than they're used to.

Brandon changed jobs in order to accommodate the 'adventure family' lifestyle and continues to thrive with his web designing job.

There are a few negatives. Nichole writes, "As a family we are learning how to be around each other all the time. I'm probably the one having the hardest time with it. So I take myself out on a date once a week and Brandon and I are regular daters so it's getting better.

They have enjoyed trying the southern cuisine like black-eyed peas, fried okra and fried shrimp but now they are sick of fried foods and chain restaurant fare.

They are finding that their plan to spend about a month in each local around the country is working out well. "The sunshine starts to wear off at about week three and a half, and then we leave and go somewhere new. We spent 5 weeks in Texas and we discovered that was too long in one place. Four weeks has been perfect. There's been a lot more growth and stretching for me. But that's what I wanted. That's what we both wanted."

Only in America, God bless it.

Bruce children watching the captain cast the fishing nets on Wolf Bay

Onboard the USS Alabama

Beth M Stephenson

Chapter 47   A Message From the Ghost of Christmas Future

Christmas is over. The Ghost of Christmas Past has claimed another year's memories. The Ghost of Christmas Presents is appearing in the form of credit card bills and tipsy scales.

This column is the Ghost of Christmas Yet to Be. Mrs. Stephenson will explain.

I found a rolled paper tucked into my door jamb a few weeks before Christmas. It spoke of people in my area who were hungry and cold. They have few resources. The family who had left the tell-tale scroll requested that instead of the usual neighborhood gifts of treats and crafts and ornaments, neighbors bring them non-perishable foods. A cardboard box was decorated on their front porch. They promise to deliver the donations to the community food bank.

Not only is it far easier than baking cookies and making candy, it protects my figure, too.

Another neighbor collected new pillows and blankets for 127 needy people. What a nice service to find those in need and deliver the largess in behalf of generous neighborhoods.

I belong to a Facebook group called an indoor garage sale. People in our town can buy and sell with pictures and prices from the comfort of home. One woman posted her plan to sell all the stuff she no longer wanted to pay for Christmas gifts. A couple of weeks later, I noted that many others had used her idea and successfully funded Christmas without using any plastic money.

I propose a strategy that will almost guarantee a relaxed and easy holiday season when it rolls around sooner than expected.

Beth M Stephenson

According to data collected by Rakuten Marketing, as many as 75% of Christmas gifts will not be kept. The majority of rejected gifts will be donated, another percentage will be re-gifted and almost 17% of holiday gifts will be resold by the recipients. While it might smack of ingratitude in December, January Christmas shoppers call it opportunity.

January is a great time to shop for engagement rings or fine jewelry on ebay. Will someone complain that a lovely diamond, millions of years in the forming, was briefly owned by another human? The same is true of almost anything material! Much of the Christmas reselling still boast their original tags.

Department store clearance shoppers are similarly clever. The lovely, soft robes or clever toys that were so enticing before Christmas seem boring and extraneous after the holiday. But when the weather chills next fall, their charm will return. Why not buy, store and resurrect these budget-friendly purchases for next year? Surely there's room under your bed to store them!

Even with my neighbors requesting non-perishable goods for the needy, I also wanted to surprise some of my neighbors with some special treats. I found this recipe for super easy, fast and delicious chocolate fudge.

In a microwave safe bowl, combine three cups of semi-sweet or milk chocolate chips, ¼ cup of butter and one can of sweetened condensed milk. Microwave on high for 1 ½ minutes, add a teaspoon of vanilla and then stir until smooth. I put chopped walnuts in the bottom of a greased 8x8 pan but you can skip the walnuts if you don't like them. Smooth the fudge into the pan and place in the fridge for about an hour to fully set. It will be smooth and delicious and it is almost impossible to ruin. It's as good as any you can buy, in my opinion.

For my fantastic holiday caramel recipe, go to my blog at www.chocolateCreamCenters.com.

Our kids have grown up and have given us grandkids. I hear other grandparents worrying about what brand or style will please their grandchild and I believe it's an exercise in futility. It's a rare grandparent that successfully identifies the exact style of clothing or gadget their grandchild yearns for. I find that young kids love kits.

My best received kit was the Handy Dandy Candy Making kits I put together for one grandson and another granddaughter several years ago. I bought candy molds online, printed recipes for jelly candies, and centers for chocolates with instructions. I included all the tools they would need and all the ingredients. They both had a ton of fun creating treats for themselves and their families. The key is to order all the parts of the kits well in advance.

So the Ghost of Christmas Future says to prepare now. Find the special something in after-Christmas sales, thrift stores and from online resellers. Buy the resold gifts at a fraction of their value long before the Christmas rush. Americans can keep the Ghost of Christmas Presents at bay,

Only in America, God Bless it.

Beth M Stephenson

Chapter 48   Food, Glorious American Food

I recently spent a couple of weeks in Ecuador, and earlier this year, we visited Asia and other Central American Countries. Everywhere we went, the average American was far richer than the average citizen of that nation.

I know Americans are often depicted as loudmouthed and fat, sporting Hawaiian shirts and oversized sunglasses. But, whether we deserve our reputation or not, if we are overweight, we come by it honestly. We have the best food!

We're used to the abundance and availability of everything we want for a recipe. French Fries are American. American pizza is merely a distant relative to the food by the same name in Italy. The Italians do gelato extremely well, but we have the best ice-cream in the world.

We, of the USA, are like a giant fondue pot, mixing the flavors, customs and traditions from all over the world. But as I've travelled the globe, it strikes me that Americans take the foods from everywhere else and make them better. I've been to Thailand, and enjoyed the food, but some of the best Thai food I've ever had was in a restaurant in downtown Salt Lake City. It was run by native Thai people who have Americanized their recipes.

Nobody that has ever been to Mexico can argue that we Americans couldn't teach the natives a few things about how to make a better taco. If a corn tortilla stuffed with meat is tasty, isn't it much tastier with sour cream? Better yet, throw some chopped tomato, avocado and cheese on there and you have something really fine!

The falafel I ate in Greece was not nearly as tasty as the falafel I had in Long Beach, CA. The French pastries we had on the French island of Saint Martin were delectable, true, but they cost ten times more than similar offerings from the bakery around the corner in my hometown.

I do have to admit that the termites I ate in Ecuador and the silk worms I ate in Thailand truly were the best I've ever eaten. Sometimes it's sensible to leave well enough alone.

Of course my observations are completely anecdotal, but even so, we Americans generally like to take any good international dish and make it sing on our lips and dance on our tongues.

Of course there are customs that improve with Americanization. I remember when I was a young teen and the Latino group from our Church wanted to have a Christmas party at our home. No Latin party is complete without a piñata, and I was eager to experience the authentic variety.

The piñata was a donkey shape adorned with bright tissue paper. They hung it from a rafter in our garage and we supplied a baseball bat. I don't think we realized that a broomstick was the usual weapon against a piñata. It was attached to a rope and we raised and lowered it while one child after another struck out.

Finally, the athletic superstar took his turn. He swung like the World Series hung on a single pitch. The bat met the paper mache' and blasted it into shreds of cardboard shrapnel. There was no scramble. There was nothing to pick up. The contents were shattered into a million bits of coffee-flavored sugar, too small to identify.

I know it was coffee candy because I could smell it. The Mexican lady who had supplied the piñata had never thought to supply wrapped candy. Maybe that was an individual error, but I have been suspicious of genuine ethnic traditions ever since.

Of course the root of the Americanization of international food is our access to hundreds or even thousands of ingredients. Instead of creating a menu from a list of 15 basics as would be typical of most countries, we have the best of everything from every part of the world available to use here. The very mixing of ingredients from the different cultures and cuisines from around the world creates a hybrid cuisine that is uniquely American.

At the new year, we tend to put away our holiday indulgences with shame. Our Hawaiian shirts are popping buttons. We have been overwhelmed by the very abundance we have celebrated. The dentists will drill out our sweet tooth and we'll endure it humbly, knowing we earned it.

But then again, we'll shed the guilt before long and move forward, relishing the variety and interest of American-style cuisine.

Only in America, God bless it.

Lunch at George's Greek Café in Long Beach

Beth M Stephenson

Chapter 49   A Great American Hero

Sometimes the greatest heroes are never widely known. William Still was one of those, known mostly by historians for the records he kept. But his story is one of daring and sacrifice. He risked his life in the cause of freedom.

He was born in New Jersey, the youngest of 18 children. His father, Levin, had earned his freedom by his hard labor. His mother, Sydney had escaped slavery twice. The first time, she and her four children made it to New Jersey where the family was reunited. But the slave catchers caught up with her and brought her back.

But Sydney craved freedom so desperately that she thwarted her master's strategy and escaped again. This time, she knew that she would never make it with all four children. The older two were boys and she reasoned that they had a better chance to survive and find their way out of slavery than her younger girls. She left the boys, Levin Jr and Peter and fled.

The family stories of heart wrenching sacrifice motivated the youngest Still to become a station master on the Underground Railroad.

It was neither Railroad, nor underground. It got its name from a slave catcher who when the runaway slave he was chasing disappeared, declared, 'It's as though he disappeared on an underground railroad.' The name and motif stuck.

It was a secret network. Nobody knew much about the other operators. Code names and passwords protected those who risked their lives helping their countrymen to freedom. Letters sent by US mail referred to runaways as 'cargo'. William Still operated the busiest station of all in his home in a busy section of Philadelphia.

One slave succeeded in shipping himself to Still's home in a wooden crate. But the runaway publicized the feat so widely, even giving interviews to reporters, that when his white helper who had shipped him tried it again, he was arrested and spent the next 8 years in prison for aiding runaways. Secrecy before, during, and after was the key to success.

But Willliam Still's own mother's yearning for her lost sons showed him that family separations were worse than physical torture, grueling labor or the humiliations of the auction block. He began a secret record, carefully documenting the stories of escapes, name changes, places of origination and destinations.

When the Fugitive Slave Act of 1850 was passed, it became legal for slave catchers to come into free states and capture runaways. They needed no warrant and if accused, even free blacks had no legal recourse. The punishment for aiding runaways or impeding the efforts of slave catchers was officially imprisonment. But the retaliation inflicted by slave catchers was much more deadly.

Most of the Underground Railroad Station Masters destroyed their records to protect themselves and those who had passed through. Though the Congress expected the FSA to halt the Underground Railroad, it had the opposite effect. Since free states were no longer safe for fugitives, the lines of the Railroad extended further north to Canada. One line ran through Niagara Falls and another through Detroit.

Even with the heightened threat, William Still kept his records, hiding them each day in an underground crypt. He actively served escapees for about 15 years until the Civil war made the Underground Railroad obsolete.

One day, an older man came into his office. The visitor's name was Peter Frieman. He told Still his story. He had been a young boy enslaved in Maryland. His mother, Sydney had escaped with her four children and been recaptured. He told of being kidnapped shortly after that and sold to a plantation in

Alabama. His father was named Levin. He explained that his older brother, Levin Jr had been whipped to death.

William cried, "What would you say if I told you that I was your brother?" A little later, Peter was reunited with his mother after being separated for 49 years.

As many as 800 people passed through William Still's Station.

After the Civil war, William Still published his records as 'The Underground Railroad: A Record of Facts, Authentic Narrative, Letters, narrating the Hardships, Hair-breadth Escapes and Death Struggles of the Slaves in their efforts of freedom as related by themselves and others or witnessed by the author, together with sketches of some of the largest stockholders and most Liberal aiders and Advisers of the Road, by William Still.

He died a wealthy man at the age of 81, a true American hero.

Only in America, God bless it.

William Still

Beth M Stephenson

Chapter 50   Chihuly Art Riots with Color and Form

A visit to Grandma's house had a different twist when I was a kid. My mother's mother (Gommy to us), tried to fend off our hooliganism by sitting us down with her large leather-bound art book and explaining the virtues of each Renaissance artist.

It worked, in a way. I grew up to believe that art is an important reflection of the society that produces it. Not only do the media used in art suggest something of the circumstances of the artist, but also the reason they produced the work of art.

My husband, Jeff, likes to arrive (inordinately) early for most events. So I found myself wandering downtown OKC one day, waiting for the theater to open for a travelling Broadway musical. The nearby art museum was closing, but there in the window, two stories high, was a structure made all of glass. The intense oranges and yellows stunned me. I stopped in my tracks. "What is THAT?" I wondered.

The identifying plate visible through the window informed me that it was art glass by Chihuly. I stood staring at it, conjuring visions of fantastical underwater gardens and magical lands. It was not only beautiful, but interesting and original. I wondered how it was structured, assuming it's mass to be too great to be self-supporting.

Alas, Gommy would have been disappointed in me. Though I remembered gawking at the giant glass sculpture, until I found the Chihuly Art Glass museum and garden on the Seattle CityPass, I had not thought to investigate further.

It turns out that Dale Chihuly is the granddaddy of a new art form. Though glass blowers and glaziers have been creating beautiful windows and objects of utility and beauty for millennia, symmetry was always the standard measure of value. Dale Chihuly changed all that.

A native of Tacoma, Washington, Chihuly studied interior design in college. He first began to innovate with glass when he began interweaving shards of stained glass into textile weaving classes. His early art glass was heavily influenced by Native American weaving patterns.

When I saw that first Chihuly pillar, I loved it for the way it made me feel. It reminded me of happy memories of snorkeling and finger painting. It struck me as an uninhibited expression of joy.

Chihuly says of his art, "I want people to be overwhelmed with light and color in some way that they've never experienced."

As I gawked my way through the Seattle Chihuly museum immediately adjacent to the Space Needle, I felt like I had entered a wonderland. The various displays indoors are mostly presented in dark rooms with the art glass backlit. There are glass gardens like a Gurney's catalog on steroids. There are undersea installations where the undulating glass suggests the drawing board of Earth's creation. Some displays are on the floor, others are at eye level and an entire gallery displays the art overhead.

Visitors move from the indoors to the outdoor gardens. The forms are vaguely reminiscent of Dr. Seuss. Though I felt like I should wear the intellectual smirk of an art aficionado, I found myself first grinning and then laughing as I moved from one area to the next.

With Dale Chihuly, there are no rules, but only the laws of nature. Nature is seldom symmetrical and so neither are Chihuly glass creations. He says that he creates art with the vision of how and where it will be viewed in mind.

A quick wander through the inevitable gift shop suggested that any art glass I purchased would not be created by Dale

Chihuly. We found a delightful art glass studio downtown the next day and bought a brilliant yellow Christmas ornament that reminded me of Chihuly's colors for a small fraction of the cost.

On ebay, the least expensive genuine Chihuly you can buy is an 8" Chihuly vase/art piece for a mere $5500.

I wonder what my ladylike Gommy would have thought of this American artist. She took up oil painting in her 60's and became a proficient copier. But I never saw any sign of unconventional joyful creativity. I may be promoting hooliganism when I show my own grandkids Dale Chihuly art glass, but I want them to enjoy it anyway. He's part of our American heritage.

Only in America, God bless it.

Enjoying the colorful exhibits at the Chihuly Museum

The Space Needle as seen from the museum, & the outdoor garden (below).

Chapter 51   Cultures of the Amish

The USA has often been called a melting pot, with world cultures blending together to make a unique American stew. While it is certainly true of our cuisine, there are elements of our society that while distinctly American, are also distinctly different.

The Amish and Mennonites are uniquely American while living in a culturally different way than most of the population. Like the people we call pilgrims, Anabaptist ancestors came to America to escape religious persecution and aggressive governments in the 17th century. Though the term Anabaptist was applied generally as a nickname because of their Christian belief that only converted adults should be baptized, the term is often used to describe a variety of sects that came from Switzerland and Germany. The Amish broke away from the larger Mennonite group because they believed in shunning those who had been excommunicated. Other doctrinal disagreements led to further dissection of culture.

Mennonites first built their agricultural communities in Pennsylvania and other eastern colonies. As large cities grew, concerns over urban influences and rising prices of land caused them to seek new lands in rural areas.

Even today, Mennonites and Amish are called the Plain People because they seek a simple lifestyle, strict Biblical adherence including simple dress. Though some segments of these societies use modern transportation and machinery, others range from using minimal technology to almost none at all. Some small pockets even repudiate electricity and plumbing.

Since some of my ancestors resided in Lancaster, PA for a few generations, I was particularly interested to visit that area. On a trip to visit our son's family in Philadelphia, we chose the exit for a town called Intercourse, mainly for the sake of the inevitable jokes.

Healthy animals grazed in the lush pastures. Trim barns and neat, two story houses nestled against the hills in self-satisfied prosperity. Well-tended fences lined the country roads and quaint shops invited us to stop. Here and there a horse and buggy trotted past.

The teenage girls working in the bakery where we stopped were simply dressed, their long hair twisted into a bun at the nape of their necks. Their ankle-length cotton dresses and white aprons were neat and apparently hand sewn of manufactured fabric. They were smiling and friendly, cheerfully using an electronic cash register and accepting a very high price for our purchases.

Amish are typically shy of being photographed because they consider photos graven images forbidden in the Bible. But I wished I had snapped a photo of the sign on the side of a black, horse drawn buggy advertising rides for $10 a head anyway. There's nothing evil about capitalism, after all.

Several years earlier, I had visited the Amish and Mennonite Amana Colonies in Iowa.

They mainly grow pork in that area of Iowa, but we saw plenty of fields of towering corn, powerful draft horses and old-fashioned farm equipment. Clean laundry wafted on the clotheslines behind the houses and birdsong stirred the quiet afternoon.

We stopped at several shops along the rural road way. The women and older girls also wore long skirts, aprons, with a prayer cap covering their hair. Men usually wear beards.

Proprietors in the various shops were friendly without being overbearing. Each answered my questions frankly and simply. They seemed content.

The Amish and that region are particularly famous for their quilts. Though dozens of styles, patterns, and color schemes are on display, traditional Amish quilts usually have a black background with bright geometric patterns made of solid colored fabric. They are tightly stitched because they are intended to be used as bedding rather than for display.

We visited a woodwork shop that was a wonderland of handmade furniture, decorations, toys and useful items.

An Amish country store boasted a huge variety of cheeses, spices, jams, meats, baked goods and delicious ice cream.

Visitors are wise to verify that a souvenir is locally made because not all shops limit themselves to handmade or locally made wares.

German is still commonly spoken in most Mennonite and Amish communities. Restaurant and bakery menus strongly favor typical German fare. Meals are generally hearty and simply prepared. Who knew that wienerschnitzel is a breaded and fried veal cutlet?

It's difficult to escape the scent of capitalism in tourist-oriented areas of Mennonite and Amish communities, but the peace of the countryside and the gentleness of the locals is a treat worth tasting.

Only in America, God Bless it.

Amish horses (above) & an Amish woodcarving we purchased in Iowa (below).

Chapter 52   Bruce Adventure Family Enjoying Winter on the Beach

Last October, the Bruce family loaded essentials into their minivan and set off on a new adventure. Their plan to travel the United States, having as many diverse experiences as possible, strengthening family bonds and learning about America is turning out well.

They stay a month in each of their rental houses, and have now gotten into a groove for wherever they go.

Since Brandon works from wherever home happens to be, he needs some level of privacy. Daily meetings and consultations require quiet, so the family plans quiet times in their homeschool routine to accommodate him as well as the family. In Santa Rosa Beach, FL, a piece of patio furniture served as a desk and a large closet worked well as an office. In their current home in Orlando/Kissimme they bought a desk off Craigslist for $15 which they will leave behind when they go.

Though the homes where they have stayed have all been a bit snug for a family of 6, they have found that some have offered a completely different lifestyle. In Santa Rosa Beach, they were close to town and the older boys loved the freedom of being able to walk to a movie or to the store. Beach excursions are common and water activities are usually a daily event.

Ironically, they had planned to spend the holiday season in Florida for the joy of being out of the cold and snows of home. But for three weeks of their stay, a record-setting cold snap dropped temperatures 30 degrees below normal.

Christmas was low key. They spent it skyping with family and going to the beach. In recent years, Nichole and Brandon had decided to give their children experiences rather than stuff for

Christmas and in that mindset, and given the fact that they were already in Florida, the main gift for the whole family was a Caribbean cruise.

It was hard for them to wait three weeks after Christmas to receive the gift, but when the time finally came, the family loved it. Though Nichole and Brandon had anticipated that the children would miss their friends as they spent this year travelling, until the cruise, they had not realized how much the children miss being with kids their own age.

They enrolled immediately in the shipboard kids' activity area and made friends with other children in that area right away. By the end of the cruise they had friends all over the ship.

One stop on the cruise was at the US territory of St Thomas in the Virgin Islands. Though lush with tropical splendor, the white beaches are several miles from the harbor. With tourist taxies being expensive, Brandon decided that the family would do like the locals do and ride the bus. Of course the bus took longer and dropped them a distance away from their destination. As they walked along the roads, they were drenched by a sudden downpour. But the beach was spectacular.

The beaches of St. Thomas are lined with reefs close to shore. Sea fans, anemones, sea urchins, brilliantly colored fish and other exotic-seeming corals seethe in the warm sea.

A few years ago, Jeff and I also enjoyed snorkeling off the beach at Secret Harbor St. Thomas, at the recommendation of our daughter-in-law. We also enjoyed snorkeling at Emerald Beach on the other side of the island. The scenery above the water is not as spectacular at Emerald Beach as at Secret Harbor, but the snorkeling was even more terrific.

I stayed out a little longer than the rest of the family and saw a reef shark between me and the beach. I remember it like a cartoon where my legs were moving so fast they were nothing but a rotating blur as I made a dash for shore.

Nichole says so far, Seaside Florida is at the top of her list to return to for a visit. In a couple of weeks, they will leave the Orlando area and move on to Hilton Head South Carolina. Both sets of grandparents are coming to visit them at Hilton Head.

They are hoping to explore Savannah GA, Charleston SC and Tybee Island GA.

Only in America, God Bless it!

ABOUT THE AUTHOR

Americana is Beth M. Stephenson's third newspaper column. It has been appearing in newspapers and online since January of 2016.

She has had a couple of novels published and has several historical fiction manuscripts in the works or ready for publication. She also writes travel articles.

When she's not writing, she's traveling the nation looking for future stories, travelling the world, curled on a couch with a book, researching for her novels, or puttering in her garden, kitchen or craft bench.

She and her husband Jeff have seven children, a girl and six boys and currently 16 grandkids. Of all her interests' her family holds supreme place in her life and heart.

She earned her Bachelor's degree in English and American Literature from Brigham Young University. She and Jeff currently live in Saratoga Springs, UT.

Made in the USA
Lexington, KY
28 May 2018